SCOTT FORESMAN · ADDISON WESLEY

Mathematics

Grade 1

Enrichment
Masters/Workbook

PEARSON

Scott
Foresman

Editorial Offices: Glenview, Illinois • Parsippany, New Jersey • New York, New York

Sales Offices: Parsippany, New Jersey • Duluth, Georgia • Glenview, Illinois
Coppell, Texas • Ontario, California • Mesa, Arizona

Overview

Enrichment Masters/Workbook enhances student learning by actively involving students in different areas of mathematical reasoning. Activities often involve students in real-world situations, some of which may have more than one right answer. Thus, the masters motivate students to find alternate solutions to a given problem.

How to use

The *Enrichment Masters/Workbook* is designed so that the teacher can use it in many different ways.

- As a teaching tool to guide students in exploring a specific type of thinking skill. Making a transparency of the worksheet provides an excellent way to expedite this process as students work at their desks along with the teacher.

- As an enrichment worksheet that challenges and motivates students to hone their thinking skills.

- As independent or group work.

- As a homework assignment that encourages students to involve their parents in the educational process.

ISBN 0-328-04932-8

2 3 4 5 6 7 8 9 10 V084 09 08 07 06 05 04 03

Table of Contents

Table of Contents continued

Oops!

Find the mistake in each pattern.
Put an X over the mistake and draw
the correct shape above.

1.

2.

3.

4.

5. Draw a pattern. Ask a friend to look for any mistakes.

Pattern Pairs

Look at the pattern of shapes and the pattern of letters. Draw the next shape. Write the next letter.

1.

○ ○ ○ ○ ○ ○

  ○   ○   ○

A   B   A   B   A   B   _____

2.

□ □ □ □ □ □ □ □ □

□ □   □ □   □ □

□   □   □

X Y Z X Y Z X Y Z _____

3.

○ □ □ ○ □ □ ○ □ □

A B B A B B A B B _____

4.

▯ ▯ ○ ▯ ▯ ○ ▯ ▯ ○

X X Y X X Y X X Y _____

Bracelet Patterns

Make a bracelet pattern. Use the shapes at the left.
The number inside each shape tells how many you
have. The pattern must repeat 3 times and use all of
the shapes.

1.

2.

3.

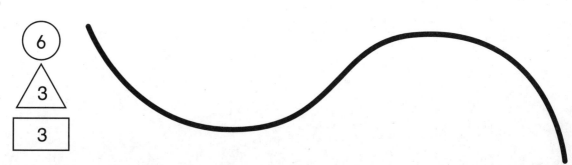

Pond Life

The number on each animal tells how many of
each live in the pond. Circle the two groups that
make up that number.

1. |

2. |

3.  |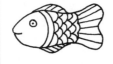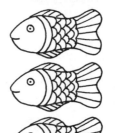

4.  |

Pack the Backpack

The number on the backpack tells how many objects it can hold. There are some objects in each backpack. Draw a line to the group of objects that will fill each backpack. Write the numbers.

1.

8 is 2 and _____.

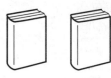

2.

9 is 4 and _____.

3.

8 is 5 and _____.

4.

9 is 7 and _____.

Play Ball

There are 10 children on the team. Each child must have a cap, a bat, and a ball.

1. Draw white counters to show how many more bats are needed.

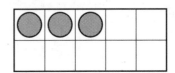

The team needs _____ more bats. 10 is __3__ and __7__.

---

2. Draw white counters to show how many more balls are needed.

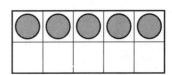

The team needs _____ more balls. 10 is _____ and _____.

---

3. Draw white counters to show how many more caps are needed.

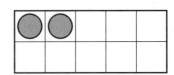

The team needs _____ more caps. 10 is _____ and _____.

© Pearson Education, Inc. 1

Name _____

At the School Store

Your points are given at the left. You must
spend all your points at the school supply store.
Circle the 2 objects you can get.

1.

| 11 points |

 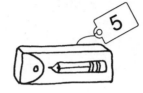 

2.

| 11 points |

 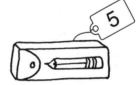 

3.

| 12 points |

 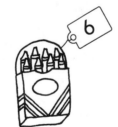 

4.

| 12 points |

Stamp Collection

Circle the 3 stamps in each row that show 12.

1. 4 3 2 5 8

2. 7 9 4 6 2

3. 2 7 1 3 5

4. 1 7 3 6 4

IN-OUT Math Machines

Numbers are missing from the Math Machines.
Write the missing numbers for each machine.

1.

IN   OUT

_____ and 2 more is 10

2.

IN   OUT

_____ and 1 more is 2

3.

IN   OUT

3 and 2 more is _____

4.

IN   OUT

5 and 2 more is _____

5.

IN   OUT

9 and _____ more is 11

6.

IN   OUT

7 and _____ more is 9

7.

IN   OUT

10 and _____ more is 12

8.

IN   OUT

6 and _____ more is 8

Name _____

One-to-One

Each person gets one object.
How many more or how many fewer are needed?
Circle **more** or **fewer** and write the number.

1.

_____ more   _____ fewer | _____ more   _____ fewer

2.

_____ more   _____ fewer | _____ more   _____ fewer

3.

_____ more   _____ fewer | _____ more   _____ fewer

Favorite Pet

The bar graph shows the number of children
who have each pet.

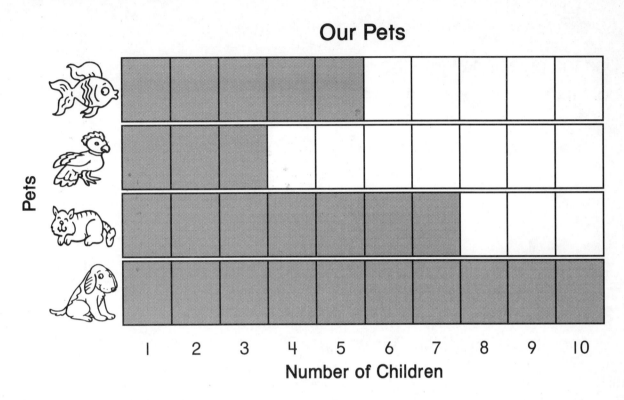

Circle the word to complete the sentence.

1. 10 is _____ than 7.   greater   less

   _____ children have dogs than cats.   More   Fewer

2. 3 is _____ than 5.   greater   less

   _____ children have birds than fish.   More   Fewer

3. 5 is _____ than 10.   greater   less

   _____ children have fish than dogs.   More   Fewer

Team Shirts

These numbers came from the team shirts.

12   4   3   5

Use the clues and write the
correct number on each shirt.

1. The number on Dan's shirt is the least.

2. The number on Tim's shirt is 2 more
   than the number on Dan's shirt.

3. The number on Sally's shirt is
   the greatest.

4. The number on Meg's shirt is between
   the number on Dan's shirt and the
   number on Tim's shirt.

Traditional Patterns

These are Japanese Kokeshi dolls. They were first made about 150 years ago in Japan.

1. Draw to continue the pattern on this doll. Color the pattern if you like.

2. Draw your own pattern on this doll.

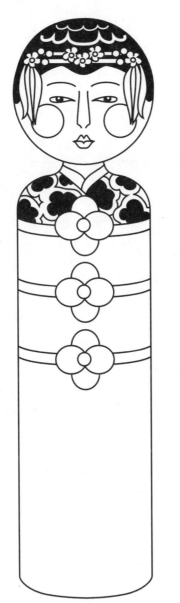 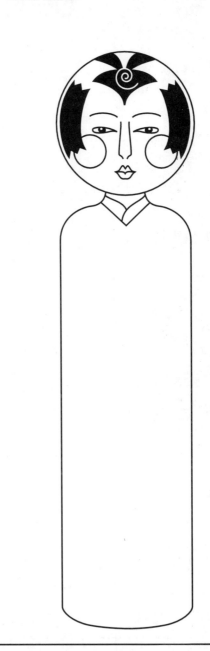

3. Look at your pattern in Exercise 2.

How many times does the pattern repeat? _____

Fall Fun

Bess and Jamie saw these objects on a Fall day.
Use their pictures to finish the table.

Bess Saw

Jamie Saw

Objects	How many did Bess see?	How many did Jamie see?	How many in all?
1. 🍂	3	0	3
2. 🐦	____	____	____
3. 🐿	____	____	____
4. 🎃	____	____	____
5. 🌰	____	____	____

Mix the Cards

Use the number cards to fill in the missing numbers.
You can use the numbers more than once.
Use counters if you like.

1. ☐ and ☐ is 10 in all.

_____

2. ☐ and ☐ is 5 in all.

_____

3. ☐ and ☐ is 8 in all.

_____

4. ☐ and ☐ is 6 in all.

_____

5. ☐ and ☐ is 4 in all.

_____

6. ☐ and ☐ is 7 in all.

_____

7. ☐ and ☐ is 9 in all.

Name _____

What Can It Be?

Add. Write the sum.

1. $3 + 0 =$ __3__   C

2. $1 + 1 =$ ____   B

3. $2 + 3 =$ ____   E

4. $2 + 2 =$ ____   O

5. $7 + 1 =$ ____   M

6. $3 + 4 =$ ____   W

7. $4 + 2 =$ ____   L

8. $7 + 2 =$ ____   T

Look at the letter next to each sum.

Write the letter above the number of the sum.

Solve the riddles.

9. What has teeth but no mouth?

A   __C__ ____ ____ ____
     3   4   8   2

10. What gets wet as it dries?

A   ____ ____ ____ ____ ____
     9   4   7   5   6

What If?

Draw a line to make a true sentence.
The first one is done for you.

I. If $2 + 0 = 2$,   then $0 + 6 = 6$.

2. If $0 + 5 = 5$,   then $9 + 0 = 9$.

3. If $4 + 0 = 4$,   then $7 + 0 = 7$.

4. If $0 + 7 = 7$,   then $5 + 0 = 5$.

5. If $0 + 9 = 9$,   then $0 + 4 = 4$.

6. If $6 + 0 = 6$,   then $0 + 2 = 2$.

7. Write your own sentence.

If _____, then _____.

Step Right Up

Climb the steps to the tower door.
Find the sum.
Add down. Add across.

1.

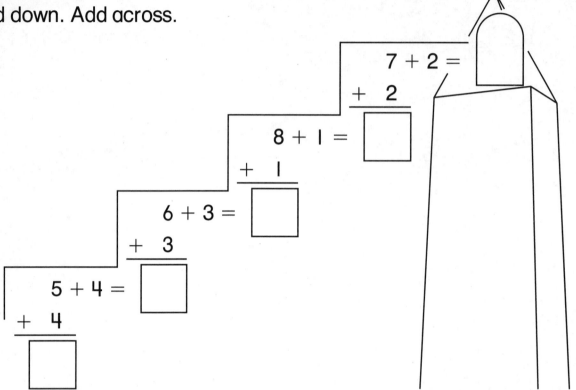

$7 + 2 =$
$+ \ 2$

$8 + 1 =$
$+ \ 1$

$6 + 3 =$
$+ \ 3$

$5 + 4 =$
$+ \ 4$

2.

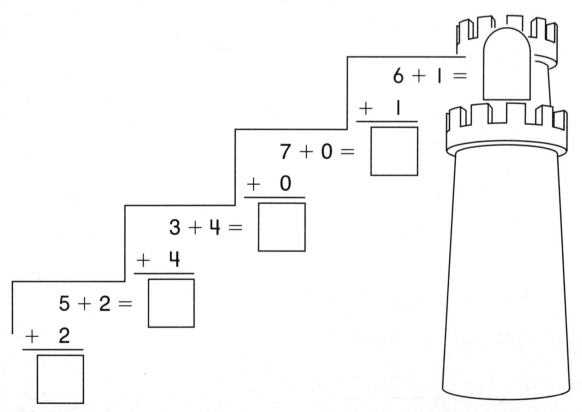

$6 + 1 =$
$+ \ 1$

$7 + 0 =$
$+ \ 0$

$3 + 4 =$
$+ \ 4$

$5 + 2 =$
$+ \ 2$

The Pet Store

Write an addition sentence to answer the question.
Circle **yes** or **no**.

1.

How many stars do you have?

_____ + _____ = _____

Do you have enough stars
for a turtle?

yes　　　　　no

2.

How many stars do you have?

_____ + _____ = _____

Do you have enough stars
for a cat?

yes　　　　　no

3.

How many stars do you have?

_____ + _____ = _____

Do you have enough stars
for a dog?

yes　　　　　no

4.

How many stars do you have?

_____ + _____ = _____

Do you have enough stars
for a rabbit?

yes　　　　　no

Tree Tales

Finish the story about the tree.
Use the picture to help you.

I. 6 birds are in the tree.

_____ birds fly away.

_____ bird is in the tree now.

2. 5 squirrels are in the tree.

_____ run away.

_____ squirrels are left in the tree.

3. 7 apples are on the tree.

_____ apples fall off the tree.

_____ apples did not fall off.

Using Coins

How many coins were used?
Write the numbers.

You have	You take away	You have left
1. _____	_____	_____
2. _____	_____	_____
3. _____	_____	_____
4. _____	_____	_____

What Will You Draw?

Complete the subtraction sentence.
Draw a picture that shows the subtraction.

1.

$5 - 1 = \underline{}$

2.

$6 - 2 = \underline{}$

3.

$4 - 3 = \underline{}$

4.

$7 - 5 = \underline{}$

Box It

Use the numbers in the box.

Write a subtraction sentence with 0 left.

Then write a subtraction sentence where all are left.

I.

3	0	3

_____ − _____ = _____

_____ − _____ = _____

2.

0	I	I

_____ − _____ = _____

_____ − _____ = _____

3.

6	6	0

_____ − _____ = _____

_____ − _____ = _____

4.

7	0	7

_____ − _____ = _____

_____ − _____ = _____

5.

0	5	5

_____ − _____ = _____

_____ − _____ = _____

Name _____

Step On It!

Step on it and drive away!

Find the difference.

Subtract across. Subtract down.

1.

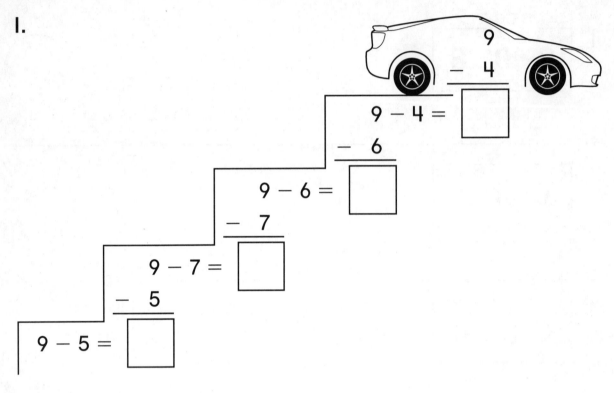

$$9 - 4 =$$

$$9 - 6 =$$

$$9 - 7 =$$

$$9 - 5 =$$

2.

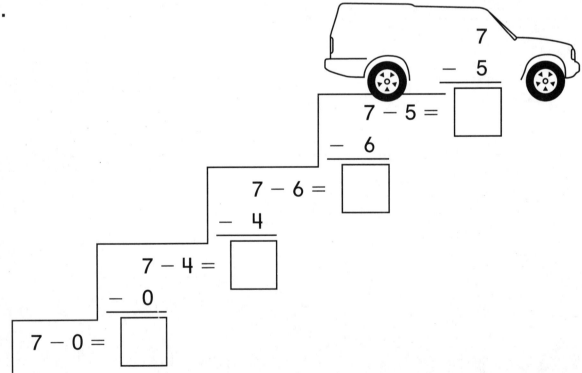

$$7 - 5 =$$

$$7 - 6 =$$

$$7 - 4 =$$

$$7 - 0 =$$

Moving Along

Felipe and Bess play a game.

The player on the greatest number at the end, wins.

To find the winner, circle **add** or **subtract**.

Write the answer.

1. Felipe starts at 1.
He moves 5 spaces.
What number is he on?

   add   subtract

   He is on ____

2. Felipe picks a card.
It says, "Go Back
3 spaces." What
number will he be on?

   add   subtract

   He will be on ____

3. Now Felipe moves to 8.
How many spaces did
he move?

   add   subtract

   ____ spaces

Bess starts at 1.
She moves 7 spaces.
What number is she on?

   add   subtract

   She is on ____

Bess picks a card.
It says, "Move to 11."
How many spaces did
she move?

   add   subtract

   She moved ____ spaces

Bess picks another card.
It says, "Go back 6 spaces."
What number is she on?

   add   subtract

   She is on ____

Who is the winner? _____

Favorite Movies

The bar graph shows the number of children who
liked each movie.

Movies We Like

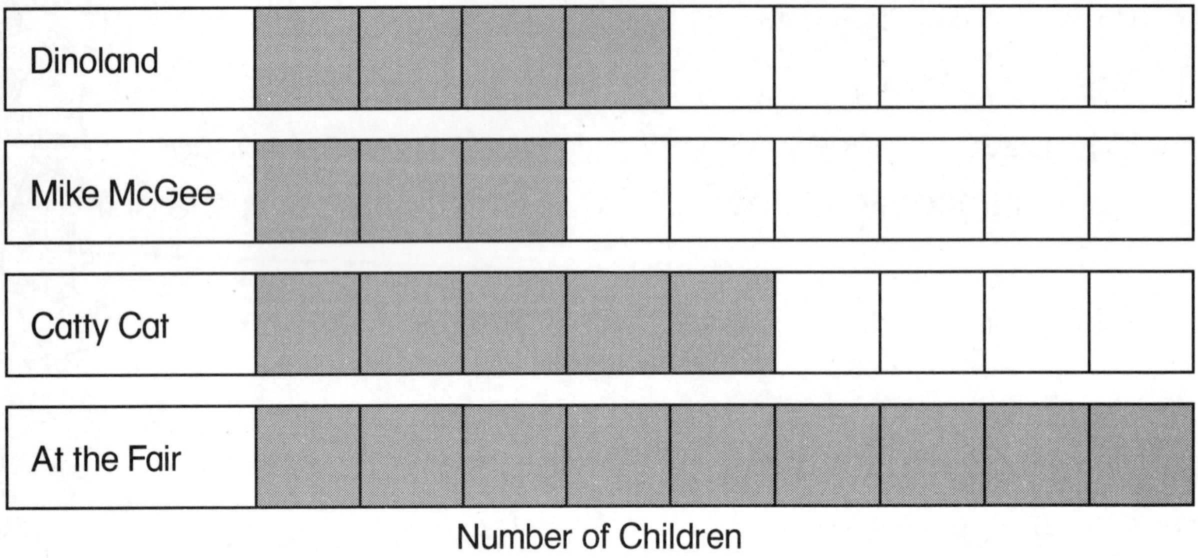

Dinoland									
Mike McGee									
Catty Cat									
At the Fair									

Number of Children

Write how many children liked the movie.
Then write how many more or how many fewer.

1. _____ Dinoland

_____ Catty Cat

_____ fewer liked Dinoland

2. _____ At the Fair

_____ Mike McGee

_____ more liked At the Fair

3. _____ Mike McGee

_____ Dinoland

_____ more liked Dinoland

4. _____ Catty Cat

_____ At the Fair

_____ fewer liked Catty Cat

Feed the Animals

Each animal gets 1 thing to eat.
Circle your answers.

1. Do the horses need more or fewer?

   2 fewer   2 more

   1 fewer   1 more

---

2. Do the rabbits need more or fewer?

     1 fewer   2 more

   4 fewer   2 more

Bug Stories

Use the picture to answer the questions.

I. _____ bugs chew on a leaf. 3 more bugs chew on a flower. How many bugs chewing are there in all?

____ ◯ ____ = ____

2. _____ bees buzz around the flower. 4 bees fly away. How many bees are left buzzing around the flower?

____ ◯ ____ = ____

3. 6 white bugs are in the grass. 8 black bugs are in the grass. How many fewer white bugs are there?

_____ fewer white bugs

4. _____ ants carry food to the anthill. 9 grasshoppers watch them. How many more grasshoppers are there?

_____ more grasshopper

Name _____

Math Machines

Write how many to add to the math machine
to get the sum.

1.

$5 + \underline{2} = 7$

2.

$3 + \underline{\hphantom{XX}} = 4$

3.

$7 + \underline{\hphantom{XX}} = 10$

4.

$9 + \underline{\hphantom{XX}} = 11$

5.

$8 + \underline{\hphantom{XX}} = 9$

6.

$6 + \underline{\hphantom{XX}} = 9$

Tree Power

Add. Circle the number sentences in each tree that
show you can add in any order and get the same sum.

1.

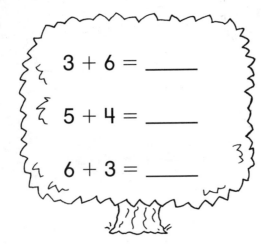

$3 + 6 =$ _____

$5 + 4 =$ _____

$6 + 3 =$ _____

2.

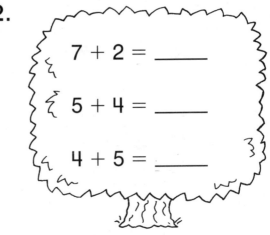

$7 + 2 =$ _____

$5 + 4 =$ _____

$4 + 5 =$ _____

3.

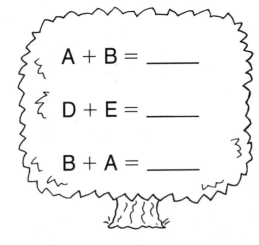

$7 + 4 =$ _____

$4 + 7 =$ _____

$6 + 5 =$ _____

4.

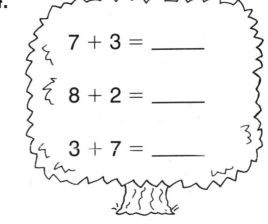

$7 + 3 =$ _____

$8 + 2 =$ _____

$3 + 7 =$ _____

5.

$A + B =$ _____

$D + E =$ _____

$B + A =$ _____

6.

$X + Y =$ _____

$Y + X =$ _____

$V + W =$ _____

Name _____

Creature Code

Use the code to find how many creatures live in the tree. Write the missing numbers.

☐ means + 3   △ means + 2   ▽ means + 1

4 ants and ☐ **3** more is __ **7** __ ants.

8 worms and △ more is _____ worms.

5 squirrels and △ more is _____ squirrels.

7 bees and ▽ more is _____ bees.

3 owls and ▽ more is _____ owls.

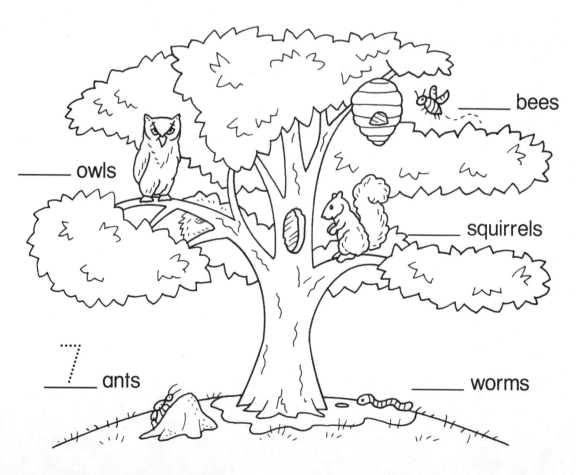

_____ bees

_____ owls

_____ squirrels

7 ants

_____ worms

Pattern Jump

Use the number line to find the pattern.
Then write a number sentence.

1.

What pattern does the number line show? ___add 1___

Write a number sentence that uses this pattern.

___5___ + ___1___ = ___6___

2.

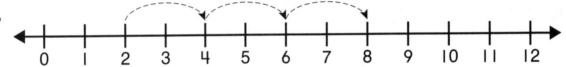

What pattern does the number line show? _____

Write a number sentence that uses this pattern.

_____ + _____ = _____

3.

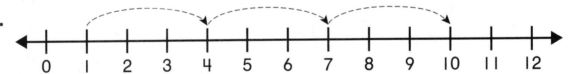

What pattern does the number line show? _____

Write a number sentence that uses this pattern.

_____ + _____ = _____

Name _____

Danny's Room

Read the story. Find the information you need to solve the problems. Then solve.

Danny cleans his room.
He finds 4 socks under his bed.
He finds 5 socks under a chair.
He hangs up 3 tee shirts and 2 striped shirts.
Then he takes a nap.

1. How many socks did Danny find?

_____ + _____ = _____ socks

2. How many shirts did Danny hang up?

_____ + _____ = _____ shirts

Danny puts away 2 basketballs.
He puts away 6 baseballs.
He puts 5 model cars on one shelf.
He puts 3 model cars on another shelf.

3. How many model cars did Danny put on the shelves?

_____ + _____ = _____ model cars

4. How many balls did Danny put away?

_____ + _____ = _____ balls

Seeing Double

Draw the double. Then write an addition sentence.

1.

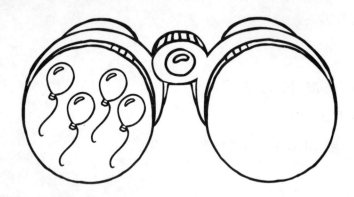

4 + ____ = ____

2.

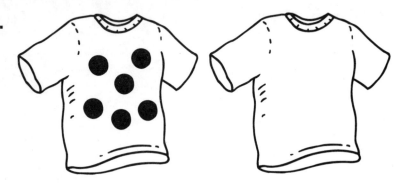

6 + ____ = ____

3.

4 + ____ = ____

4. Make your own double.

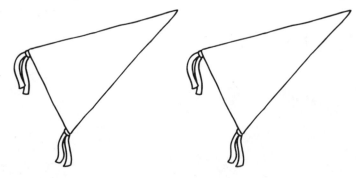

____ + ____ = ____

© Pearson Education, Inc. 1

Double Dominoes

Look at the domino. It shows a double.
Draw the domino that shows the double plus one.
Write a number fact for each domino.

1. 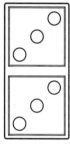  ☐ + ☐ = ☐   ☐ + ☐ = ☐

2. 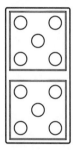  ☐ + ☐ = ☐   ☐ + ☐ = ☐

3. 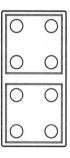 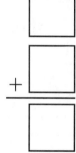 ☐ + ☐ = ☐   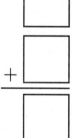 ☐ + ☐ = ☐

4. 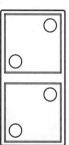 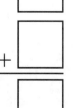 ☐ + ☐ = ☐   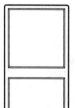 ☐ + ☐ = ☐

Ten in a Van

Each van can hold 10 children. The gray counters show how many children are in the van. Draw counters to show how many more children can fit in the van.

1.

```
┌───┐
│ 2 │
└───┘
┌───┐
│   │
+ └───┘
─────
 10
```

2.

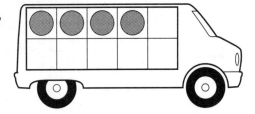

```
┌───┐
│   │
└───┘
┌───┐
│   │
+ └───┘
─────
 10
```

3.

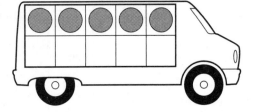

```
┌───┐
│   │
└───┘
┌───┐
│   │
+ └───┘
─────
 10
```

4.

```
┌───┐
│   │
└───┘
┌───┐
│   │
+ └───┘
─────
 10
```

Name _____

Picture This

Draw a line from the exercise to the picture you would
use to solve it. Then write a number sentence.

1. Sue picks 5 apples.
   She picks 4 more apples.
   How many apples does she pick in all?

   ____ + ____ = ____

2. Dan eats 3 apples.
   Jay eats 4 apples. How many
   apples do they eat altogether?

   ____ + ____ = ____

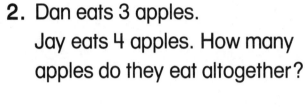

3. Tanya buys 6 red apples.
   She buys 4 green apples.
   How many apples does Tanya buy?

   ____ + ____ = ____

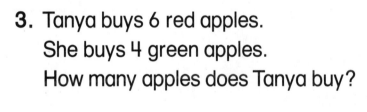

4. There are 5 apples at home.
   Tyrone brought 6 more apples home.
   How many apples are there now?

   ____ + ____ = ____

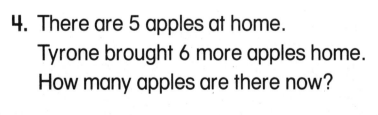

Rabbit Match

Draw a line to match the rabbit with its cage.

1. The number on Flopsy's cage is 2 more than 5.

2. The number on Long Ear's cage is the double of 4.

3. The number on Hoppy's cage is 1 more than the double of 5.

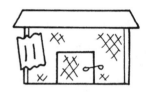

4. The number on Puffy's cage is 2 more than 8.

5. The number on Bunny's cage is the double of 6.

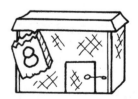

Count Back

Count back to subtract.
Use the number line if you like.

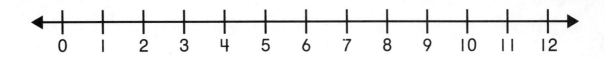

1. $9 - \underline{\hspace{1cm}} = 7$

I counted back _____.

2. $6 - \underline{\hspace{1cm}} = 4$

I counted back _____.

3. $5 - \underline{\hspace{1cm}} = 4$

I counted back _____.

4. $2 - \underline{\hspace{1cm}} = 0$

I counted back _____.

5. $11 - \underline{\hspace{1cm}} = 9$

I counted back _____.

6. $10 - \underline{\hspace{1cm}} = 9$

I counted back _____.

7. $12 - \underline{\hspace{1cm}} = 10$

I counted back _____.

8. $8 - \underline{\hspace{1cm}} = 7$

I counted back _____.

9. $7 - \underline{\hspace{1cm}} = 6$

I counted back _____.

10. $4 - \underline{\hspace{1cm}} = 2$

I counted back _____.

11. $9 - \underline{\hspace{1cm}} = 8$

I counted back _____.

12. $3 - \underline{\hspace{1cm}} = 2$

I counted back _____.

Next Stop

Everyone must get off the train by the last stop.
Only 0, 1, or 2 people get off at each stop.
Fill in the boxes at each stop.

Number of People

	On Train		Getting Off		Left
1. Stop 1	12	−	2	=	10
2. Stop 2	10	−		=	
3. Stop 3		−		=	
4. Stop 4		−		=	
5. Stop 5		−		=	
6. Stop 6		−		=	
7. Stop 7		−		=	
8. Stop 8		−		=	

Sailing with Doubles

Use the numbers on the flags to write an addition sentence and a subtraction sentence.

1.

____ + ____ = ____

____ − ____ = ____

2.

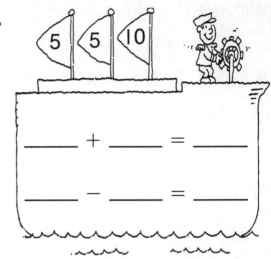

____ + ____ = ____

____ − ____ = ____

3.

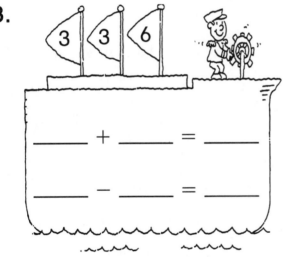

____ + ____ = ____

____ − ____ = ____

4.

____ + ____ = ____

____ − ____ = ____

5.

____ + ____ = ____

____ − ____ = ____

6.

____ + ____ = ____

____ − ____ = ____

Name _____

Animal Cards

At school the children earn points.
They trade the points for animal cards
at the school store.

 Dinosaur
8 points

 Polar Bear
7 points

Elephant
6 points

 Shark
5 points

 Lion
4 points

Monkey
3 points

Write a number sentence. Solve.

1. Dan has 10 points.
   He picks a lion card.
   How many points does Dan have left?

   $10 \ominus 4 = 6$

   Circle the other card
   Dan can get.

---

2. Lina has 12 points.
   She picks a polar bear card.
   How many points does Lina have left?

   ____ ◯ ____ = ____

   Circle the other card
   Lina can get.

---

3. Chris has 11 points.
   She picks a dinosaur card.
   How many points does Chris have left?

   ____ ◯ ____ = ____

   Circle the other card
   Chris can get.

Name _____

Related Fact Fun

Complete the addition and subtraction facts.
Then circle the two facts in each row that are related.

1. $6 - 3 =$ _____ $2 + 4 =$ _____ $6 - 4 =$ _____

2. $12 - 5 =$ _____ $7 + 5 =$ _____ $6 + 5 =$ _____

3. $6 + 2 =$ _____ $6 - 2 =$ _____ $8 - 2 =$ _____

4. $3 + 5 =$ _____ $2 + 3 =$ _____ $5 - 3 =$ _____

5. $10 - 3 =$ _____ $10 - 6 =$ _____ $3 + 7 =$ _____

6. $5 + 2 =$ _____ $6 + 1 =$ _____ $7 - 2 =$ _____

7. $9 - 4 =$ _____ $6 + 3 =$ _____ $9 - 6 =$ _____

8. $1 + 5 =$ _____ $6 - 1 =$ _____ $11 - 2 =$ _____

9. $10 - 5 =$ _____ $4 + 6 =$ _____ $10 - 4 =$ _____

10. $2 + 7 =$ _____ $9 - 8 =$ _____ $9 - 7 =$ _____

11. $2 + 5 =$ _____ $3 + 4 =$ _____ $7 - 3 =$ _____

12. $11 - 5 =$ _____ $11 - 1 =$ _____ $6 + 5 =$ _____

Fact Family Tree House

Choose one number from each toolbox to write a fact family for each tree house.

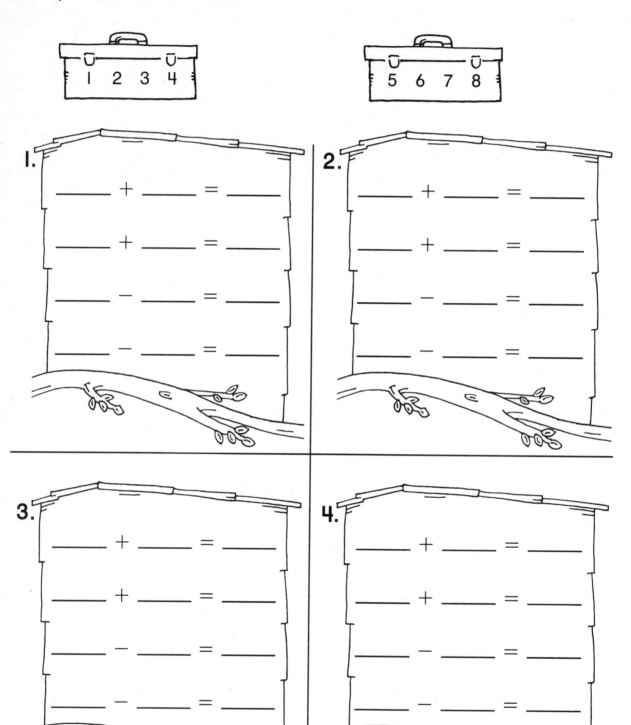

Handy Addition Facts

Solve the addition facts. Then write the subtraction
sentence that answers the question.

1.

$8 + 3 =$ _____

$3 + 5 =$ _____

Mike has 8 coins.
He gives 3 coins to Kate.
How many coins does he have left?

_____ − _____ = _____   _____ coins left

Circle the addition fact that helped you.

2.

$5 + 1 =$ _____

$6 + 1 =$ _____

Emma wants to read 7 books.
She reads 6 books.
How many more books does she need to read?

_____ − _____ = _____   _____ more book

Circle the addition fact that helped you.

3.

$6 + 6 =$ _____

$6 + 5 =$ _____

There are 11 apples.
The children eat 5 apples.
How many apples are left?

_____ − _____ = _____   _____ apples left

Circle the addition fact that helped you.

Nature Walk

Use the picture to find the animals to complete the
number sentence. Circle **add** or **subtract**.

---

1. How many more birds than
snakes are there?

add   subtract

_____ ◯ _____ = _____

---

2. How many squirrels and frogs
are there altogether?

add   subtract

◯

_____ _____ = _____

---

3. How many more butterflies
than turtles are there?

add   subtract

◯

_____ _____ = _____

---

4. How many turtles and snakes
are there in all?

add   subtract

_____ ◯ _____ = _____

Name _____

Puppy Problems

Julio has 9 puppies.

He has a box of 6 toys.

Complete the number sentence.

I. How many more toys does he need so
   that each puppy has a toy?

   _____ ◯ _____ = _____ more toys

2. Julio finds another box with 5 more toys.
   How many toys does he have in all?

   _____ ◯ _____ = _____ toys

3. Julio has 2 puppy beds.
   4 puppies can sleep on each bed.
   How many puppies can sleep on the beds?

   _____ ◯ _____ = _____ puppies

Circle the correct answer.

4. Does Julio have enough beds for his puppies?

   yes   no

5. How many beds does Julio need for his 9 puppies?

   2   3   4

On Solid Ground

Write how many of each solid figure you find in the structure.

I.

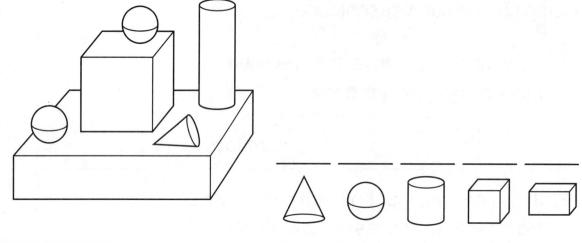

2.

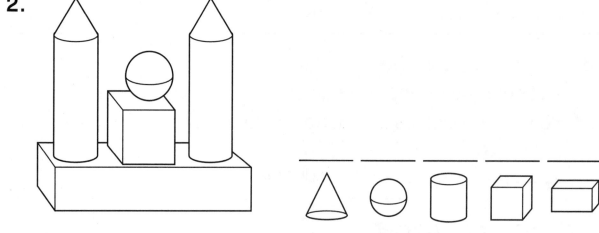

3.

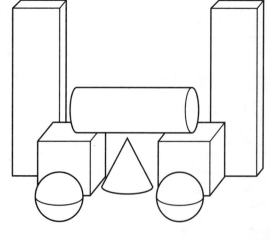

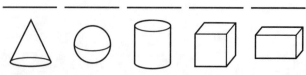

Solid Match

Draw a line to match the shape to its description.

1.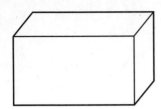

| I flat face |
| I vertex |

2.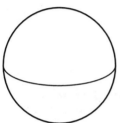

| 0 flat faces |
| 0 vertices |

3.

| 6 flat faces |
| 8 vertices |

4.

| 2 flat faces |
| 0 vertices |

5. Draw the solid figure that has 2 flat surfaces and 0 vertices.

Solid Cuts

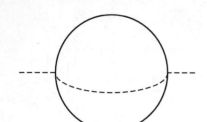

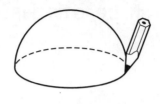

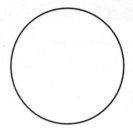

Cut a sphere.

Trace the
flat surface.

You get a
circle shape.

Look at the cut of each solid figure.
Color the shape you would get if you traced the flat surface.

1.

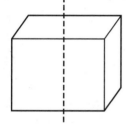 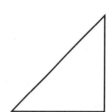 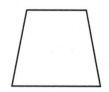

2.

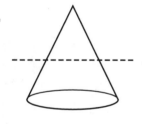   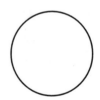

3.

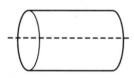 

Ship Shape

I. Color the circles red.
Color the triangles blue.
Color the squares green.
Color the rectangles yellow.

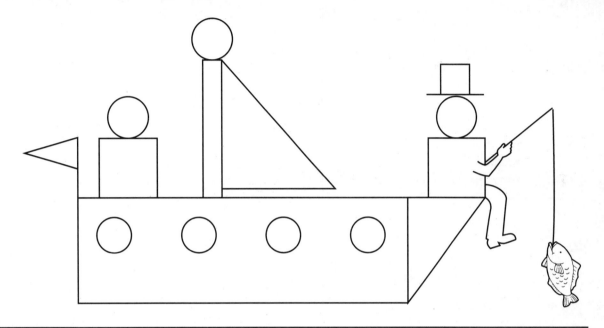

2. Draw your own picture.
Use circles, squares, triangles, and rectangles.
Color your picture.

Robot Match

Each robot is made with plane shapes.
Draw a line to match each robot to
its box of plane shapes.

1.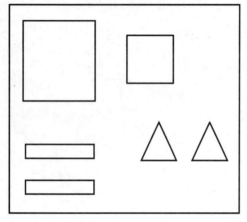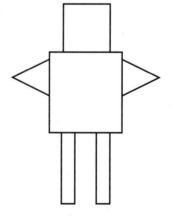

2.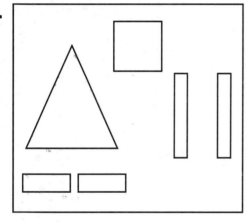

3.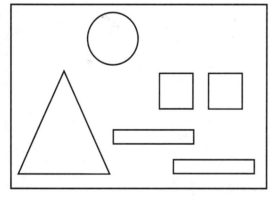

Matching Shapes

In Exercises 1–2, color the objects with the same shapes red.

1.

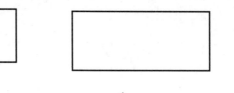
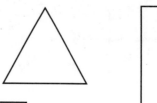

2.

Color the shapes that match green.

3.

Missing Parts

Look at each shape and the line of symmetry.
Draw the missing part.

1.
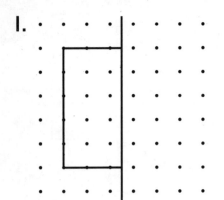

2.
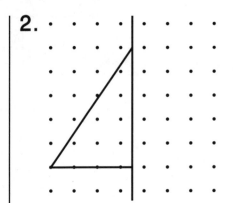

3.
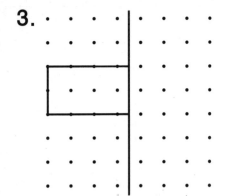

4.
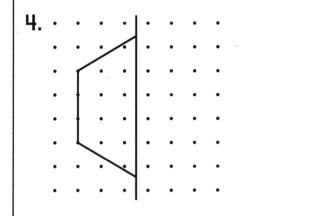

5.
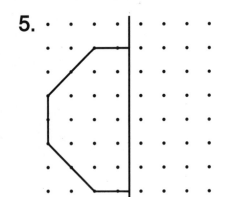

6.
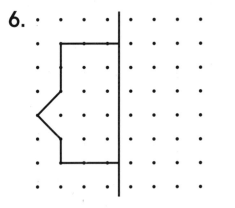

Slide, Flip, Turn

Look at the patterns.
Circle what comes next.

1.

2.

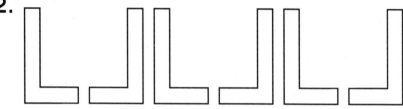
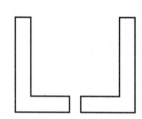

3.

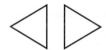

4.

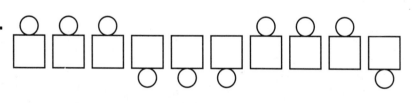

Shape Making

Use these three pattern blocks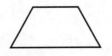
to make different shapes.

Draw a picture of the shape you make.

Write how many of each shape you used.

Shapes I Made	Shapes I Used		
	△̄	◇	△
1.			
2.			
3.			

Even Steven

Help the children share.
Draw lines to show equal parts.

1.

2 boys share an apple.

2.

3 girls share a pizza.

3.

4 children share
the sandwich.

4.

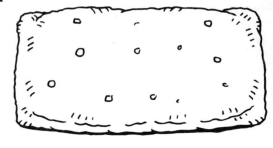

6 children share
the banana bread.

Half Time

Draw a straight line on each shape.
Show two different ways to make halves.

1.

2.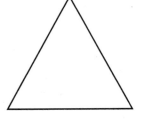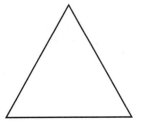

3.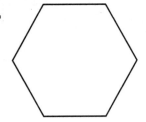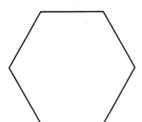

4.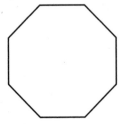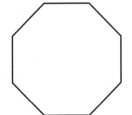

Name _____

Lunch Time

Color one part of each object.
Write the fraction that names the equal part of
the whole which you colored.

I.

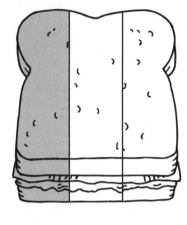

$\dfrac{1}{3}$

2.

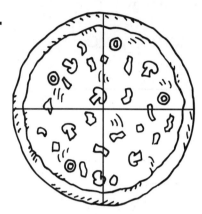

_____

3.

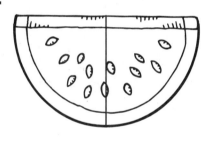

_____

4.

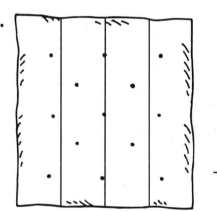

_____

5.

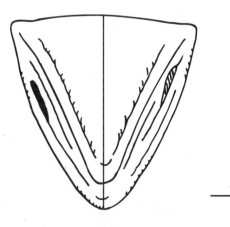

_____

6.

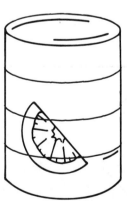

_____

Fraction Action

Draw a picture to show each story.

1. Lu has a group of

   3 tennis balls.

   $\frac{1}{3}$ of them is yellow.

2. Marco has 4 sports cards.

   $\frac{1}{4}$ of them has a picture

   of a baseball.

3. Eva has 2 backpacks.

   $\frac{1}{2}$ of her backpacks has

   a zipper on it.

Name _____

Fraction Patterns

Color to show what comes next in the pattern.
Write the fraction.

1.

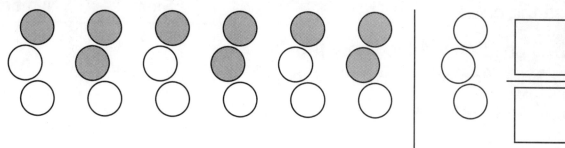

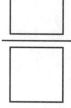

2.

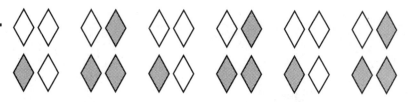

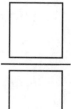

3.

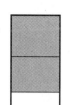 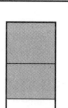 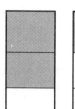 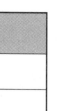 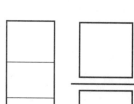

4.

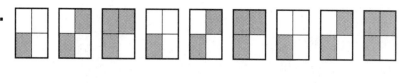

Stamp Club

Children in the stamp club share stamps equally.
Help them share the stamps.
Use the chart.

Stamp		Number
bear		6
flower		10
bird		12
dog		8

1. 3 children want to share the bear stamps equally. How many stamps will each child get?

   Each child gets _____ bear stamps.

2. 4 children want to share the bird stamps equally. How many stamps will each child get?

   Each child gets _____ bird stamps.

3. Which stamp can 5 children share equally?
   Circle the answer.

   bird   dog   flower

4. Can 9 children share the dog stamps equally?
   Circle **yes** or **no**.

   yes   no

   Draw a picture to explain. Use counters if you like.

Prize Winners

Your class is having a contest.
Design a trophy for the winner.
Use some or all of these shapes.

    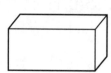

Write how many of each shape you used.

Cylinder _____

Cone _____

Sphere _____

Rectangular prism _____

Cube _____

A Minute of Your Time

Circle the pictures of the things you could do in about one minute.

1.

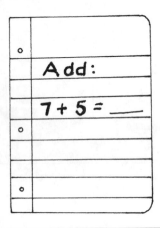

2.

3.

4.

5.

6.

Name _____

Do You Have the Time?

What is a good time to do each of these activities?
Write the time. Then draw an hour hand and a minute
hand to show the time.

1.

_____ o'clock

2.

_____ o'clock

3.

_____ o'clock

4.

_____ o'clock

Rocky's Day

Read about Rocky's Day. Draw hands on the clock face. Write the time on the other clock.

1. Rocky walks the dog at 7 o'clock.

2. Rocky plays at 10 o'clock.

3. Rocky reads at 1 o'clock.

4. Rocky feeds the dog at 4 o'clock.

5. Rocky eats 3 hours after he feeds the dog.
Write the missing time that shows when Rocky eats.

4:00, 5:00, 6:00, _____:_____, 8:00

Good Morning!

What time does Farmer Brown do each chore?
Write the letter of the clock that shows the time.
Then write the time on the other clock.

A    B    C    D

1. Farmer Brown eats breakfast
between 9 o'clock and 10 o'clock.

   A

_____

2. Farmer Brown wakes up when the rooster
crows between 4 o'clock and 5 o'clock.

____

3. Farmer Brown milks the cows between
11 o'clock and 12 o'clock.

____

4. Farmer Brown feeds the pigs between
6 o'clock and 7 o'clock.

____

As Time Goes By

Draw hands on the clock to show the starting time and the ending time. Then write how long each activity lasted.

1. Sam began reading at 5 o'clock. He stopped reading at 6 o'clock. How long did Sam read?

_____I hour_____

2. Tippy falls asleep at 1 o'clock. She naps until 4 o'clock. How long does Tippy nap?

_____

3. Dee's soccer practice starts at 10 o'clock. The practice lasts until 12 o'clock. How long does soccer practice last?

_____

4. School starts at 8 o'clock. Tom's bus is late. It doesn't get to school until 11 o'clock. How late is the bus?

_____

Activities We Like to Do

Look at each picture.
When do you like to do each activity?
Write **morning**, **afternoon**, or **night**.

1.

_____

2.

_____

3.

_____

4.

_____

5.

_____

Name _____

Are You Finished Yet?

About how long does the activity take?
Write the word **minutes**, **hours,** or **days** to answer.

1.

About 1 _minute_

2.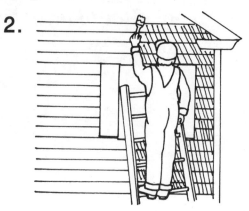

About 3 _____

3.

About 2 _____

4.

About 2 _____

5.

About 3 _____

6.

About 2 _____

Name _____

Fun at the Fair

Look at the schedule for the school fair.
Each activity comes right after the one before it.

Fair Schedule		
Activity		**Time**
	Puppet Show	11:30
	Make Your Own Bracelet	12:30
	Dig for Toy Dinosaurs	1:00
	Face Painting	2:00
	Clown Fun	2:30
	Bingo	3:30

1. List the activities that take a half hour.

_____

_____

2. List the activities that take 1 hour.

_____

_____

3. Bingo is over at 4:30.
How long does Bingo last? _____

4. Lisa leaves her house at 10:00 to go to the fair.
Peg says it will take about an hour to get there.
Will Lisa have enough time? _____

Calendar Challenge

Write the missing numbers.

July						
Sunday	Monday	Tuesday	Wednesday	Thursday	Friday	Saturday
		1	2	3		
6		8				12
		15	16			19
20				24	25	
		29		31		

Now use the calendar to answer the questions.

1. How many Mondays are in this month?

_____

2. How many Tuesdays are in this month?

_____

3. On what day is July 4th?

_____

4. What is the date of the first Sunday in this month?

_____

Mixed-up Months

Write the months in order on the calendar.

(blank)

S	M	T	W	T	F	S
		1	2	3	4	5
6	7	8	9	10	11	12
13	14	15	16	17	18	19
20	21	22	23	24	25	26
27	28	29	30	31		

(blank)

S	M	T	W	T	F	S
					1	2
3	4	5	6	7	8	9
10	11	12	13	14	15	16
17	18	19	20	21	22	23
24	25	26	27	28		

March

S	M	T	W	T	F	S
					1	2
3	4	5	6	7	8	9
10	11	12	13	14	15	16
17	18	19	20	21	22	23
24/31	25	26	27	28	29	30

(blank)

S	M	T	W	T	F	S
	1	2	3	4	5	6
7	8	9	10	11	12	13
14	15	16	17	18	19	20
21	22	23	24	25	26	27
28	29	30				

(blank)

S	M	T	W	T	F	S
			1	2	3	4
5	6	7	8	9	10	11
12	13	14	15	16	17	18
19	20	21	22	23	24	25
26	27	28	29	30	31	

(blank)

S	M	T	W	T	F	S
						1
2	3	4	5	6	7	8
9	10	11	12	13	14	15
16	17	18	19	20	21	22
23/30	24	25	26	27	28	29

(blank)

S	M	T	W	T	F	S
	1	2	3	4	5	6
7	8	9	10	11	12	13
14	15	16	17	18	19	20
21	22	23	24	25	26	27
28	29	30	31			

August

S	M	T	W	T	F	S
				1	2	3
4	5	6	7	8	9	10
11	12	13	14	15	16	17
18	19	20	21	22	23	24
25	26	27	28	29	30	31

(blank)

S	M	T	W	T	F	S
1	2	3	4	5	6	7
8	9	10	11	12	13	14
15	16	17	18	19	20	21
22	23	24	25	26	27	28
29	30					

(blank)

S	M	T	W	T	F	S
		1	2	3	4	5
6	7	8	9	10	11	12
13	14	15	16	17	18	19
20	21	22	23	24	25	26
27	28	29	30	31		

(blank)

S	M	T	W	T	F	S
					1	2
3	4	5	6	7	8	9
10	11	12	13	14	15	16
17	18	19	20	21	22	23
24	25	26	27	28	29	30

(blank)

S	M	T	W	T	F	S
1	2	3	4	5	6	7
8	9	10	11	12	13	14
15	16	17	18	19	20	21
22	23	24	25	26	27	28
29	30	31				

March	August	October	June
April	December	July	February
November	May	January	September

1. Jeri's 8th birthday is on 5/14/2004.
   Write that date another way. _____

2. It is September. Juan's birthday
   will be in two months. In which month
   is Juan's birthday? _____

At the Reptile House

Reptile House Shows		Start	Finish
 Alligator Alley		1:00	2:00
Slithery Snakes		2:00	3:00
Turtles and Tortoises		2:30	3:00
Leaping Lizards		3:00	3:30
New Baby Reptiles		3:00	4:00

Use the schedule to answer the questions.

1. What time does the Slithery Snakes show begin? Show the time on both clocks.

2. Linda sees Alligator Alley and Slithery Snakes. How long do the two shows take?

_____

3. John wants to see Slithery Snakes and Turtles and Tortoises. Can he do that?

_____

4. Alan sees the New Baby Reptiles show. There are 12 baby alligators. There are 5 baby turtles. How many more baby alligators than baby turtles are there?

_____ − _____ = _____ more

Here Comes the Sun!

Write the missing numbers.

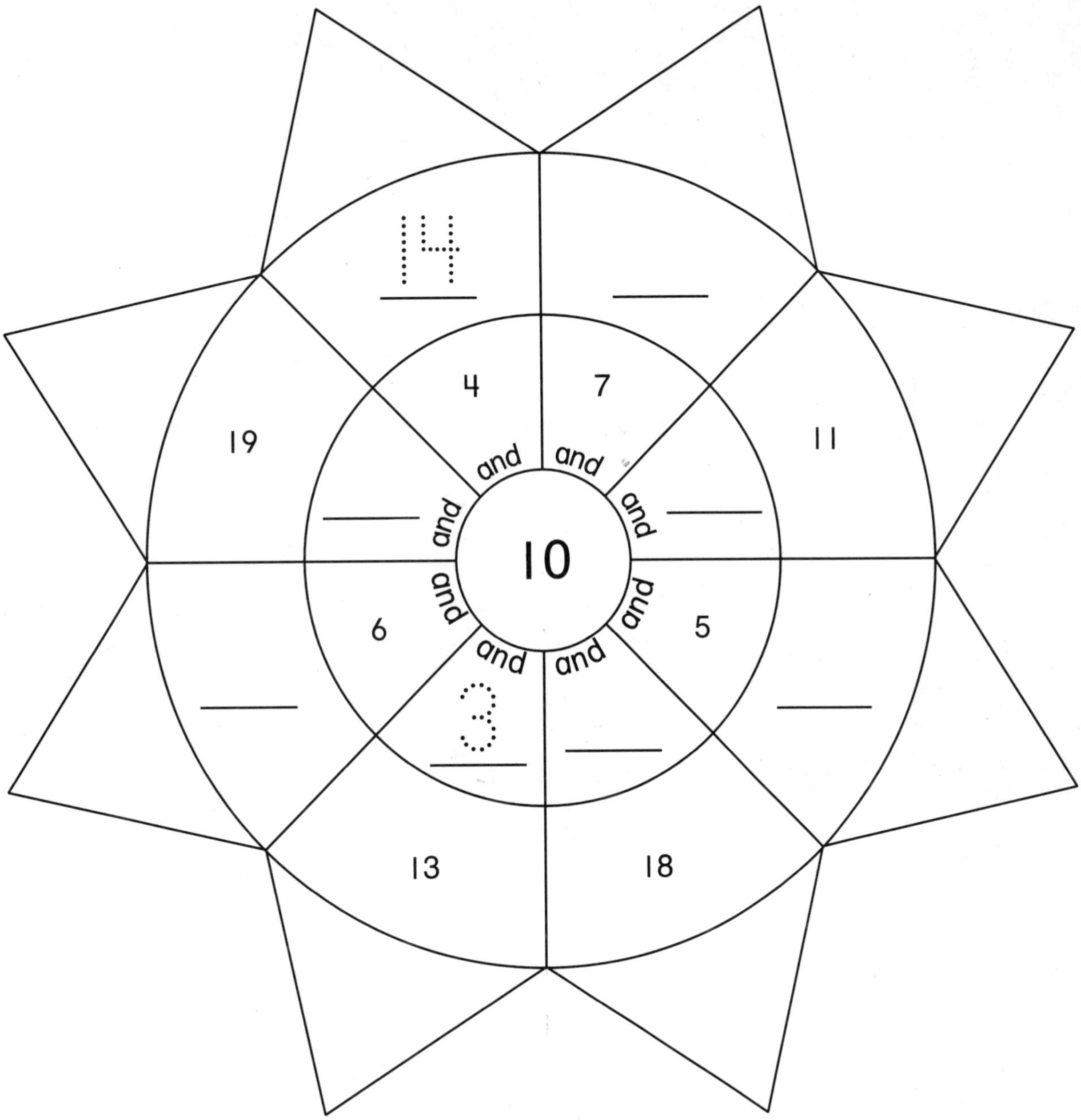

14 ___

4   7

and and
and   and
and 10 and
and   and
and and

6   5

3 ___ ___

19

11

___

___

13   18

Tens in the Barnyard

Circle groups of ten. Count by tens. Write the number.

1.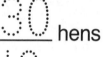

__3__ groups of ten

__30__ hens

One more group of ten would make __40__ hens.

2.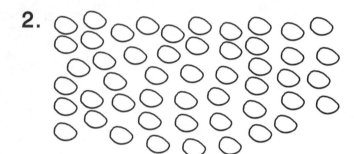

_____ groups of ten

_____ eggs

Two more groups of ten would make _____ eggs.

3.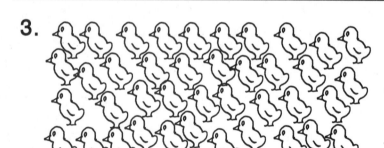

_____ groups of ten

_____ chicks

Two more groups of ten would make _____ chicks.

4.

_____ groups of ten

_____ roosters

One more group of ten would make _____ roosters.

Hundred Chart Puzzle

Write the missing numbers.
Then draw a line from a piece
on one side to another piece
that completes the puzzle.

1.

7	8		10
17		19	

14	
	25

32			35

2.

11		13	
21	22		
31			

67			70
		79	
			90
	99		

3.

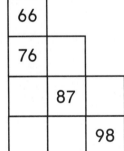

66	
76	
	87	
		98

		20
27			
37		39	

4.

71	
81	
	92	93	

	73		75
		84	
			95

Name _____

Who Wins the Puppy?

Each child has a number.
Read the clues. Write the number.

1. Dan has
   4 groups of 10 and
   3 left over.

   Dan's number is _____.

2. Nancy has
   3 groups of 10 and
   7 left over.

   Nancy's number is _____.

3. Tanya has
   5 groups of 10 and
   1 left over.

   Tanya's number is _____.

4. Manny has
   2 groups of 10 and
   9 left over.

   Manny's number is _____.

5. Amit has
   7 groups of 10 and
   4 left over.

   Amit's number is _____.

6. Jasmine has
   9 groups of 10 and
   9 left over.

   Jasmine's number is _____.

Use the clues to figure out who wins the puppy.
Write the name.

7. The winner needs more than 5 groups of 10
   and less than 6 groups of 10.

   The winner is _____.

Name ______________________________

About How Many?

E 7-5
ESTIMATION

Read the number.
Circle the group that shows about that many.

1. 30	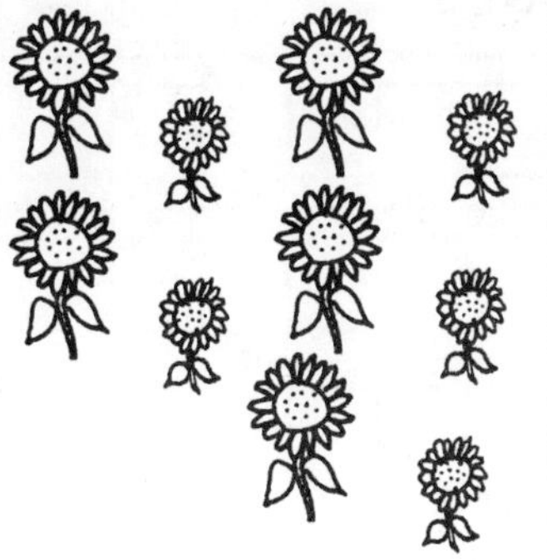	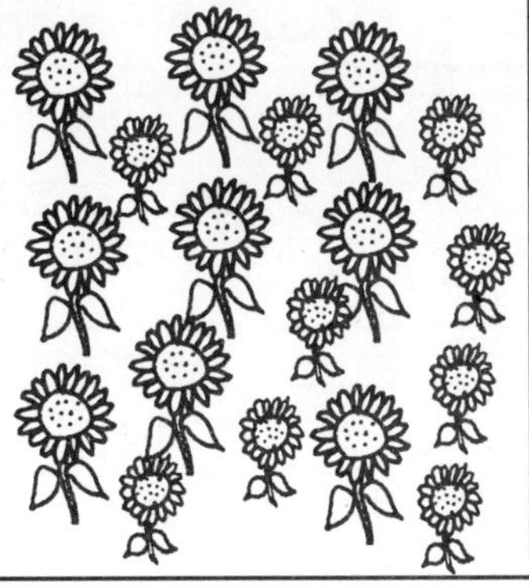	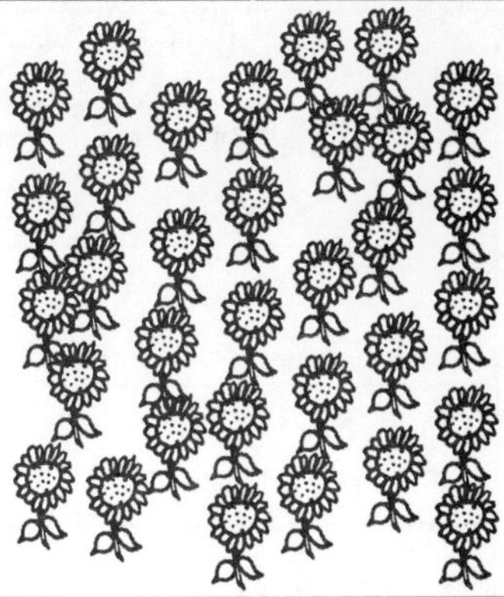
2. 20	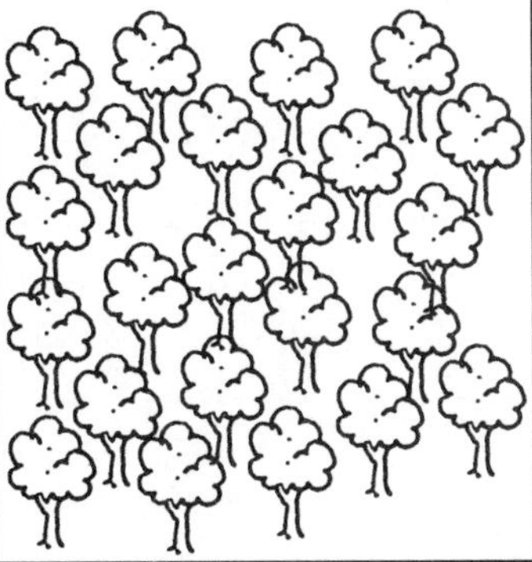	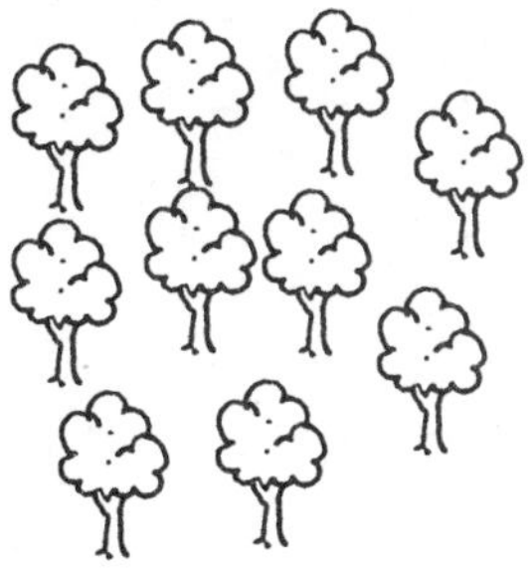	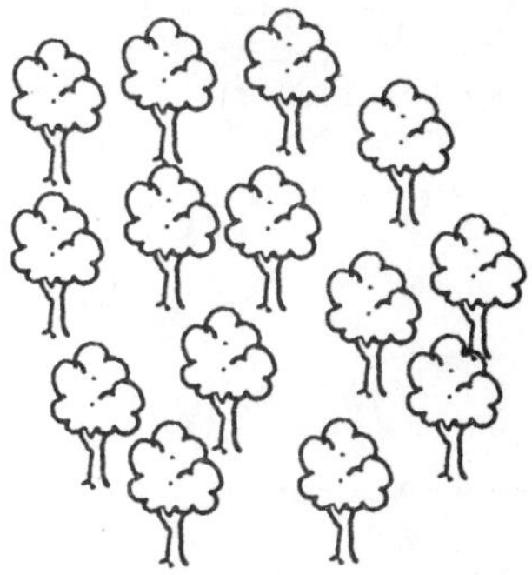
3. 50	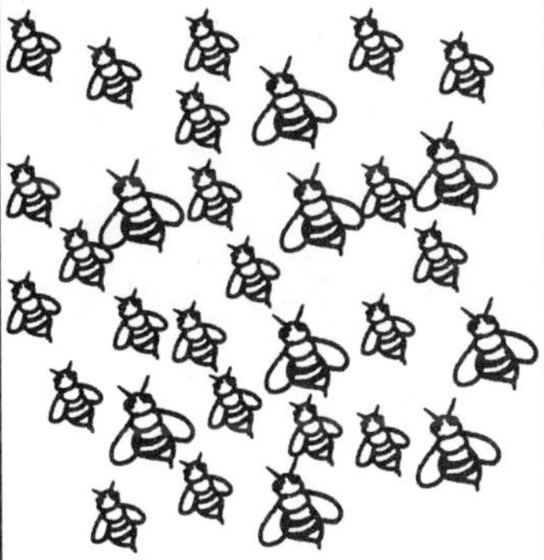	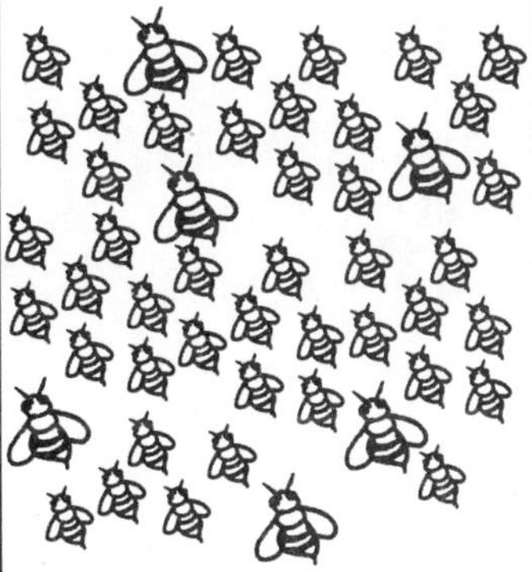	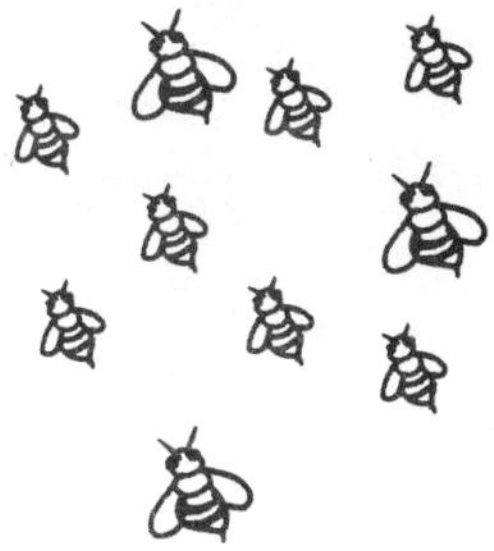
4. 40	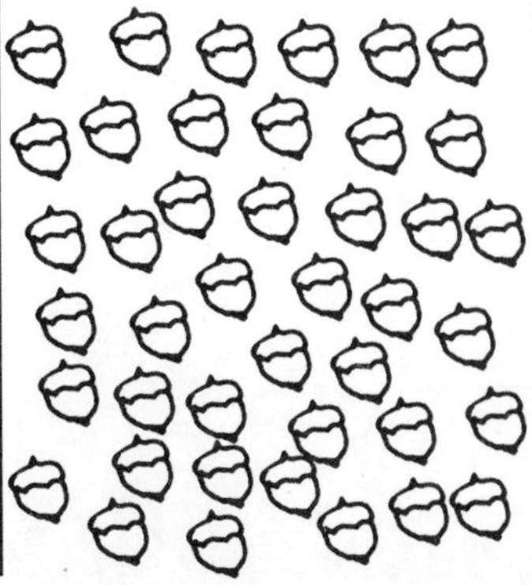	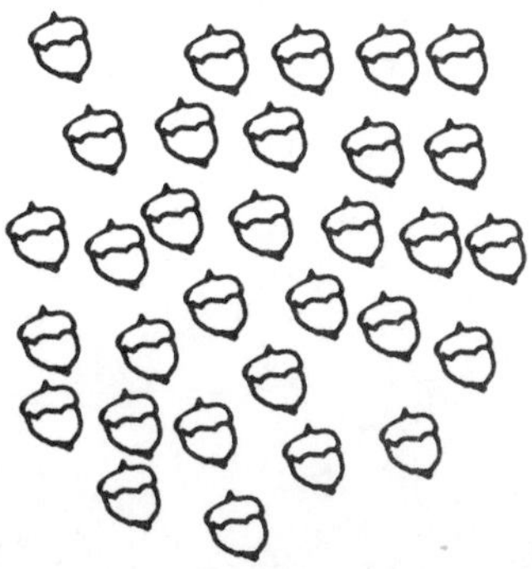	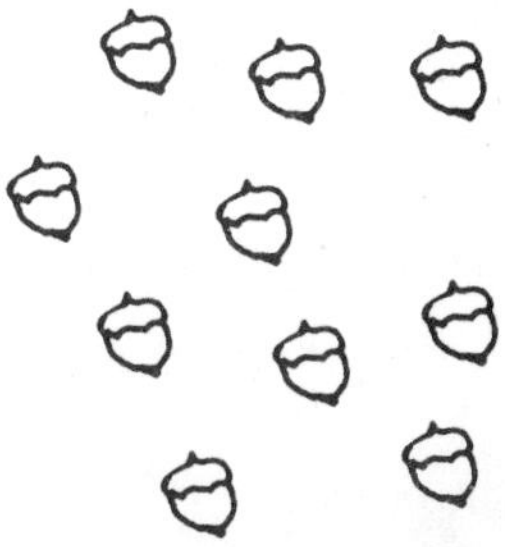

What's for Lunch?

Ask 15 children to vote for their favorite food.
Color one square on the graph for each vote.

Lunch Favorites		
Peanut Butter and Jelly Sandwich		
Vegetable Soup		
Pizza		

Use the graph to answer the questions.

1. Which food got the most votes? _____

2. Which food had the least votes? _____

3. How many votes did vegetable soup get? _____

4. How many votes did peanut butter and jelly sandwiches get? _____

5. Which food or foods got more than 10 votes? _____

Chart Patterns

Use the patterns on the chart to complete the sentences.

A	B	C	D	E
31	32	33	34	35
36	37	38	39	40
41	42	43	44	45
46	47	48	49	50

1. Write the numbers under E.

_____, _____, _____, _____

The numbers skip count

by _____.

2. Write the numbers under A.

_____, _____, _____, _____

The numbers skip count

by _____.

3. If the chart continued,
the number 55 would be

under letter _____.

4. If the chart continued,
the number 51 would be

under letter _____.

5. Under D, the next number

after 49 would be _____.

6. Under C, the next number

after 48 would be _____.

How Will You Count?

Read each exercise. Decide if you will skip count by two, five, or ten. Count. Then write the answer.

1. How many sails?

Skip count by _____.   There are _____ sails.

2. How many books?

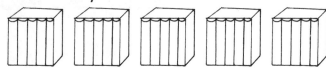

Skip count by _____.   There are _____ books.

3. How many wings?

Skip count by _____.   There are _____ wings.

4. How many pencils?

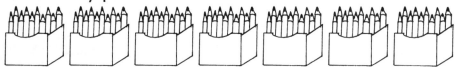

Skip count by _____.   There are _____ pencils.

5. How many balloons?

Skip count by _____.   There are _____ balloons.

Name _____

Showing Off

Jake has 20 model cars. He wants to buy
a bookcase to display them. Find a pattern.
Then write the numbers.

I. The red bookcase has 5 shelves.
   5 cars can fit on each shelf.

Number of shelves	1				
Number of cars	5				

_____ cars will fit on the red bookcase.

2. The blue bookcase has 7 shelves.
   3 cars can fit on each shelf.

Number of shelves							
Number of cars							

_____ cars will fit on the blue bookcase.

3. Which bookcase do you think Jake should buy?

   Red   Blue

   Why? _____

   _____

A Riddle for the Seasons

Write the numbers that are before, after, or between.

20	70	52	40	69	91
E	R	E	A	U	P

79	41	71	27	55
M	T	E	T	R

1. _____, 28   **2.** _____, 53   **3.** _____, 80

4. 90, _____   **5.** 19, _____   **6.** 54, _____

7. 39, _____, _____, 42   **8.** 68, _____, _____, _____, 72

Find the card with each number.
Match the letters to the
numbers on the lines below
to solve the riddle.

What goes up and down but never moves?

The ___ ___ ___ ___ ___ ___ ___ ___ ___ ___ ___!
27 52 79 91 20 55 40 41 69 70 71

Odd and Evens

Color the odd numbers red.
Color the even numbers blue.

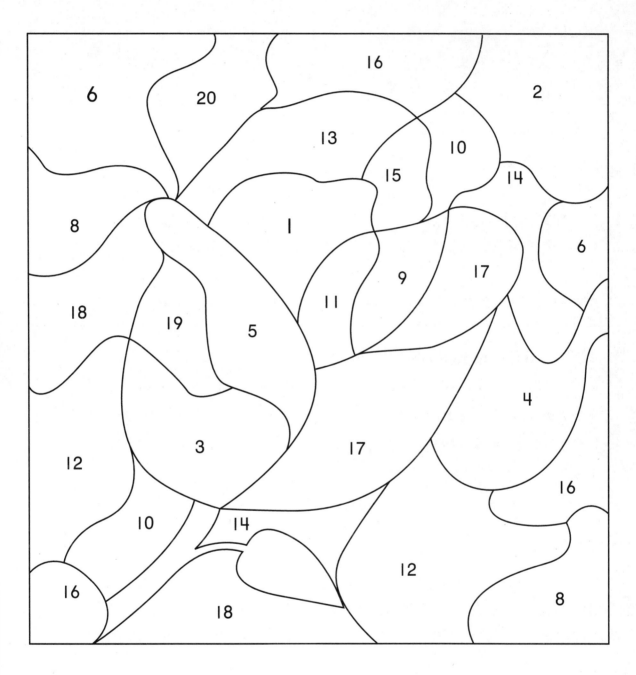

At the Pet Show

The animals line up in the order that they won.
Some prize ribbons fell off.

1. Circle the place that
   the frog won.

   seventh   ninth   eighth

2. Circle the place that
   the lizard won.

   third   fourth   fifth

3. The turtle was just ahead
   of the mouse. The mouse
   was in last place. What
   place did the turtle win?

   _____

4. The cat won the place
   between the snake and
   the dog. What place did
   the cat win?

   _____

5. Gloria's pet was ahead
   of the fish. Her pet is **not**
   the hamster. Which pet
   belongs to Gloria?

   _____

6. Jeremy's pet came in fourth.
   Mike's pet came in two places
   ahead of Jeremy's pet.
   Which pet belongs to Mike?

   _____

At the Lake

Read the exercises. Solve.

1. 5 families go to the lake.
   There are 3 children in each family.
   How many children are there in all?

Number of families					
Number of children					

_____ children

---

2. Is there an odd or even number of children in all?

   odd   even

---

3. There are 6 canoes.
   2 people can fit in each canoe.
   Skip count to find out how many people
   can take a canoe ride.

   _____, _____, _____, _____, _____, _____

4. Circle the 4th canoe.

5. Color the 3rd canoe red.

6. In what position is the last canoe? _____

Does It Belong?

Circle the one in each row that does not belong.

Write the correct number.

1. (40) 4 tens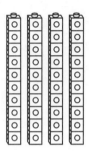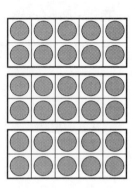

_____ tens is _____.

2. (30)  3 tens

_____ tens is _____.

3. (70) 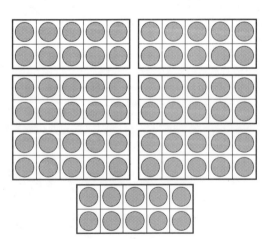 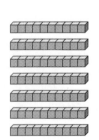 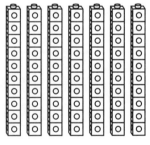 6 tens

_____ tens is _____.

At the Parade

Ten children march in each row.

Other children march in front of the rows.

Count how many children are marching altogether.

1.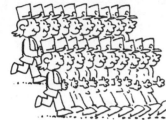

2.   _____

3. 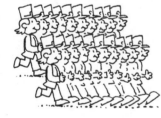   _____

4.    _____

Box the Buttons

How many buttons in Column A?

Write the tens and ones in Column B.

Match the number with the button box in Column C.

A	B	C
1.	____4____ tens + ____6____ ones	64
2.	_____ tens _____ ones	46
3.	_____ tens _____ ones	35
4.	_____ tens _____ ones	27
5.	_____ tens _____ ones	47

How Many Ways?

Write each number three different ways.

1.

Tens	Ones
3	7

37

Tens	Ones
2	17

Tens	Ones
	37

2.

Tens	Ones

44

Tens	Ones

Tens	Ones

3.

Tens	Ones

23

Tens	Ones

Tens	Ones

4.

Tens	Ones

56

Tens	Ones

Tens	Ones

5.

Tens	Ones

87

Tens	Ones

Tens	Ones

6.

Tens	Ones

61

Tens	Ones

Tens	Ones

Summer Vacation

Match the pictures to each story.
Then write the answer.

1. Marie found 27 white shells and
32 pink shells at the beach.
How many shells did Marie
find in all?

   _____ shells

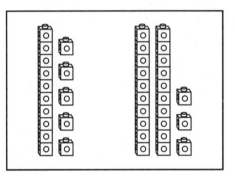

2. Rafael used two jars to catch
48 fireflies in all. He caught 27
in one jar. How many did he
catch in the other jar?

   _____ fireflies

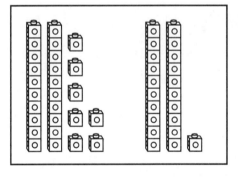

3. Lena picked 15 roses.
Then she picked 23 daisies.
How many flowers did she
pick in all?

   _____ flowers

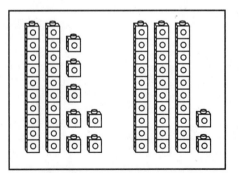

4. Jen and her mom filled two
baskets with 45 peaches in all.
Jen's basket held 30 peaches.
How many peaches were in
her mom's basket?

   _____ peaches

Jed's New Pet

Start at 20. Follow the arrows. Write the numbers.
The number in the last box will match the number on
Jed's new pet. Circle the pet.

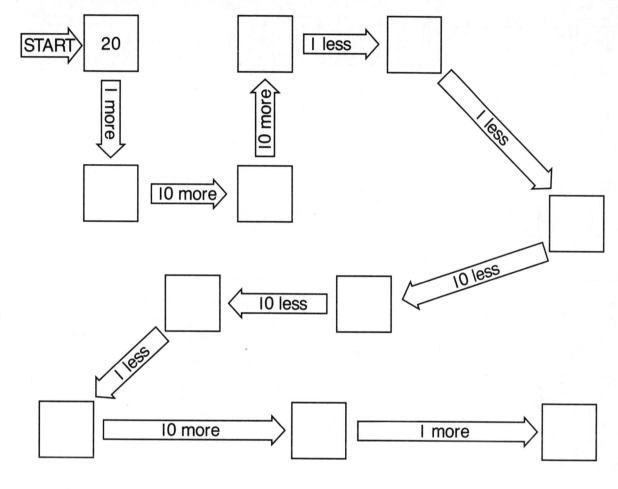

Weigh to Go

Choose two numbers for each see-saw.

Write $<$, $>$, or $=$ in the circle.

You can use each number only once.

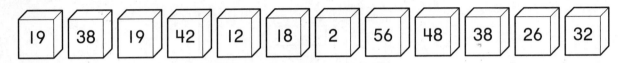

1.

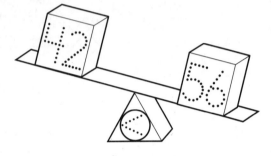

2.

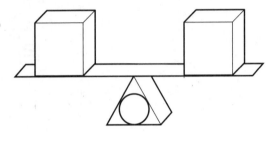

3.

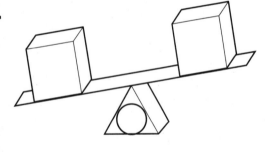

4.

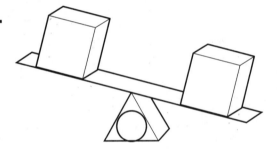

5.

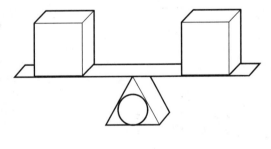

6.

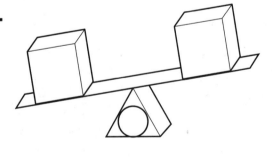

Cool Numbers

Use the numbers in the triangles to write
3 different two-digit numbers.
Write your numbers in the circles.
Then place them on the number line.

1.

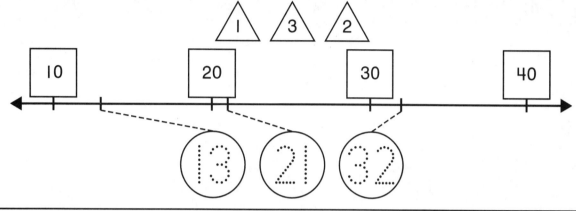

2.

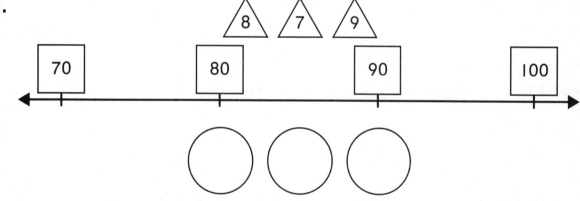

3.

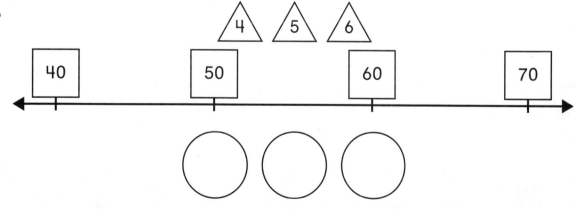

Big Fish, Little Fish

Write the numbers in order from least to greatest.

1. 27   72   45   63

least   greatest

2. 35   97   16   52   77

least   greatest

Write the numbers in order from greatest to least.

3. 40   89   65   23

greatest   least

4. 99   66   55   77   88

greatest   least

Hundreds Match

△ = 100   □ = 10   ○ = 1

Match each number to the group of objects in the box
that stand for the numbers.

1. 725

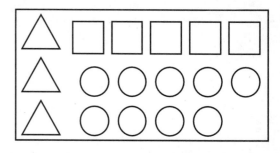

2. 1 hundred   9 tens   7 ones

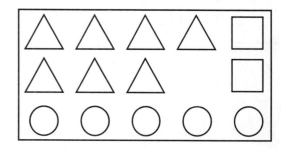

3. 359

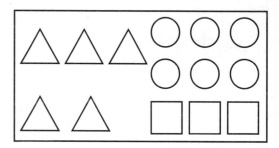

4. 5 hundreds   3 tens   6 ones

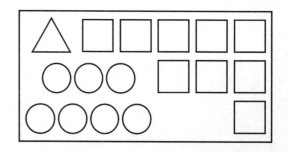

Button Sort

Sort the buttons 3 different ways. Draw the buttons.
Tell the sorting rule that you used.

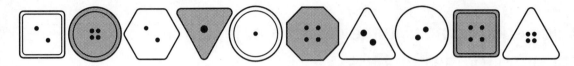

1.

Sorting Rule: Buttons _____.

2.

Sorting Rule: Buttons _____.

3.

Sorting Rule: Buttons _____.

Picture It!

Ken made a table to show the favorite vegetables of his friends. Use the table and the information below to finish the picture graph.

Vegetable		Votes
	Carrot	4
	Tomato	8
	Corn	2

Our Favorite Vegetables

Carrot								
Tomato								
Corn								

I. 6 more friends selected corn as their favorite vegetable. Show how many selected corn altogether.

2. 3 more friends selected carrots as their favorite vegetable. Show how many selected carrots altogether.

3. 4 friends decided **not** to select tomatoes as their favorite vegetable. Show how many selected tomatoes.

Use the graph to answer questions.

4. Which vegetable is the favorite? _____

5. Which vegetable is the least favorite? _____

Bars and Objects

Use the bar graph to show how many of each object.

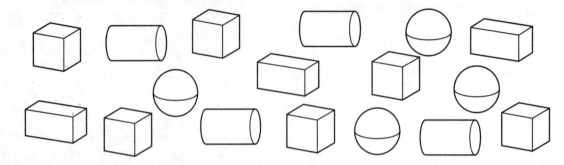

Kinds of Objects									
Cubes									
Cylinders									
Spheres									
Rectangular Prisms									
	1	2	3	4	5	6	7	8	9

Use your bar graph to answer the questions.

I. Which object is shown the most? _____

2. Which objects are shown the same number of times?

_____

3. If there were 3 more spheres, how many spheres

would there be on the bar graph? _____

4. Make up your own question about the bar graph.

_____

Tally Mark Fun

Make tally marks to show how many of each item you and a friend have altogether.

		Total
Pencil		
Eraser		
Crayon		
Coin		

Use the tally chart to answer the questions.

1. Of which item are there the most?

   _____

2. Of which item are there the fewest?

   _____

3. Are there more or fewer pencils than crayons?

   _____

   How many more or fewer?

   _____

4. How many coins and erasers are there altogether?

   _____

Fun at the Zoo

You and your family visit the zoo.
What animals will you see?

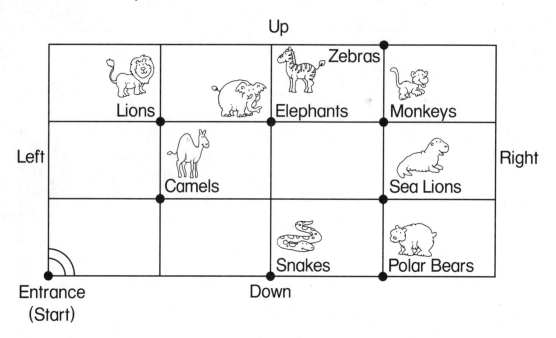

Use the map. Complete the sentences.

1. You are at the entrance. The first animals you want

   to see are the _____camels_____.

   You will go __1__ block __right__ and __1__ block __up__.

2. You visit the elephants. The next animals you want

   to see are the _____.

   You will go _____ blocks _____ and _____ blocks _____.

3. You visit the sea lions. The next animals you want

   to see are the _____.

   You will go _____ blocks _____ and _____ blocks _____.

Saturday Errands

You and your dad have three errands to do.

Find the shortest path.

Decide what you will do first, second, and third.

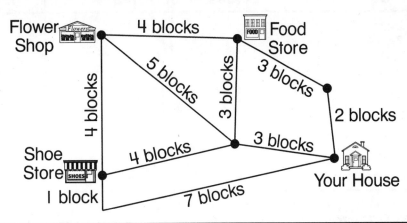

_____

How many blocks is it? Write an addition sentence.

1. From your house to the _____.

   _____ + _____ = _____ blocks.

   _____

2. From the _____ to the _____.

   _____ + _____ = _____ blocks.

   _____

3. From the _____ to the _____.

   _____ + _____ = _____ blocks.

   _____

4. From the _____ to your house.

   _____ + _____ = _____ blocks.

The Class Trip

The children voted for where they wanted
to go on the class trip. Write the totals.

Place	Number of Votes	Total
Zoo	卌 ‖	
Aquarium	卌 卌 ‖‖	
Dinosaur Park	卌 卌 卌	

I. Write the number of votes in order from the least to greatest.

_____ < _____ < _____

least   greatest

2. Which place will the class visit? _____

3. Find the shortest path from the school
   to the place the class will visit.
   Write an addition sentence.

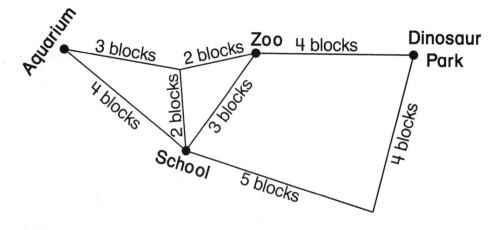

_____ blocks + _____ blocks = _____ blocks.

Shopping for Toys

Count the money in each pocket.
Write how much money in all.
Then circle the toy you can buy.

1.

_____ ¢ in all

2.

_____ ¢ in all

3.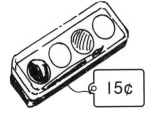

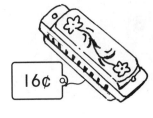

_____ ¢ in all

4.

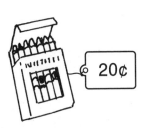

_____ ¢ in all

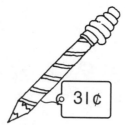

School Supplies

Look at the two items.
Circle the one you want.
Then circle the coins to match the price.

1.

21¢   31¢

2.

53¢   62¢

3.

   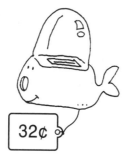

42¢   32¢

4.

   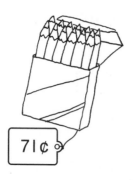

61¢   71¢

In the Bank

What color is each child's bank?
Read the clues. Color the banks.
Then draw a line from the child to his or her bank.

1. Jane's bank has 3 dimes
   and 1 nickel. Color
   Jane's bank red.

45¢

2. Eduardo's bank has
   3 dimes and 3 nickels.
   Color Eduardo's bank blue.

60¢

3. Jawan has 6 dimes
   and 1 nickel.
   Color Jawan's
   bank yellow.

35¢

4. Kim has 4 dimes
   and 4 nickels. Color
   Kim's bank purple.

65¢

Arts and Crafts

Larry uses plastic shapes to make toys.
Look at the price of each shape.

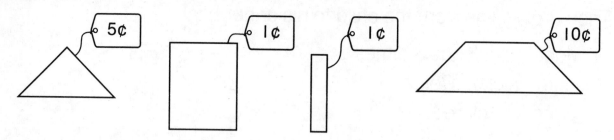

Write how much Larry spends to make each toy.

I.

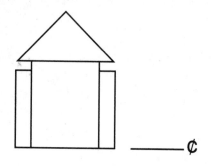

_____ ¢

2.

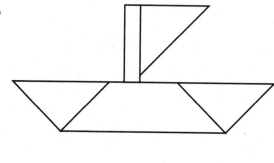

_____ ¢

3.

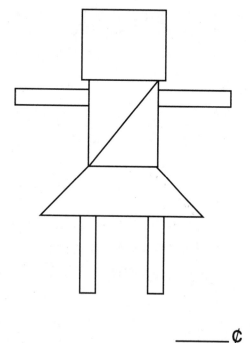

_____ ¢

4. Use the shapes to make your own toy. Write how much you would spend.

_____ ¢

What's for Lunch?

Menu

Yogurt 11¢	Apple 7¢
Sandwich 9¢	Milk 6¢
Cheese and crackers 5¢	Juice 8¢

Use the menu to figure out how much each lunch will cost. Write how much change each child will get.

1. Sally has 20¢.
   She gets yogurt
   and juice.

   She spends _____ ¢.

   Will she get change? _____

2. José has 15¢.
   He gets cheese and
   crackers and an apple.

   He spends _____ ¢.

   Will he get change? _____

3. Brian has 15¢.
   He gets a sandwich
   and milk.

   He spends _____ ¢.

   Will he get change? _____

4. Linda has 20¢.
   She gets a sandwich
   and juice.

   She spends _____ ¢.

   Will she get change? _____

Quarter Challenge

Can you show 25¢ in 8 different ways?
Circle the way that shows the fewest coins.

	Dimes	Nickels	Pennies
I. 25¢	1	3	
2. 25¢			
3. 25¢			
4. 25¢			
5. 25¢			
6. 25¢			
7. 25¢			
8. 25¢			

Bank on It!

Count the coins in each bank. Then write how much
money in all. Circle the bank in each row that has
the most money.

I.

_____ ¢   _____ ¢   _____ ¢

2.

_____ ¢   _____ ¢   _____ ¢

Share and SHARE Alike

Each child should get one dollar. Circle the coins
to show a dollar. Draw a line to each child.

Mabel

Eddy

Rick

Javier

Lucy

© Pearson Education, Inc. 1

At the Museum Store

Read each problem. Solve.
Then write an addition sentence to check your work.

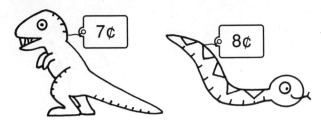 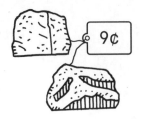 

7¢   8¢   9¢   10¢

1. Lyn spends 16¢.
She buys the rocks.
Circle the other toy she buys.

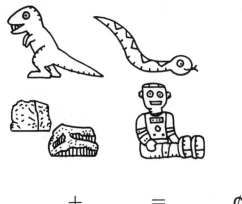

____ + ____ = ____ ¢

2. Paul spends 18¢.
He buys the robot.
Circle the other toy he buys.

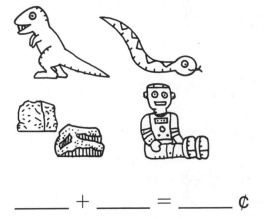

____ + ____ = ____ ¢

3. Sara spends 14¢.
She buys 2 things.
One is the dinosaur.
Circle the other toy she buys.

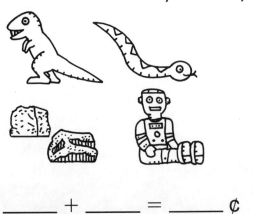

____ + ____ = ____ ¢

4. Eric spends 17¢.
He buys the dinosaur.
Circle another toy he buys.

____ + ____ = ____ ¢

Yard Sale

The children want to buy things at the yard sale.
Read each problem. Solve.

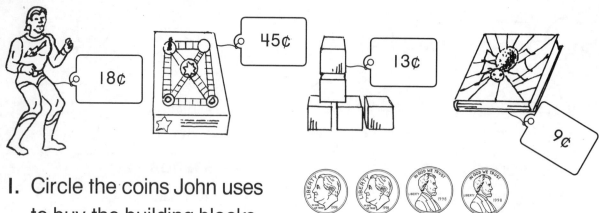

1. Circle the coins John uses
   to buy the building blocks.

---

2. Caitlin wants to buy the board game.

   The price of the board game is _____ ¢.

   Is the price an even or odd number? _____

---

3. Caitlin has 50¢.
   Circle the coins she uses
   to buy the board game.
   How much will she have left? _____ ¢

       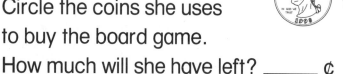

---

4. Bob buys the action figure.
   Circle the coins he uses.
   Can Bob buy the book?

   yes   no

   Will he have money left over?

   yes   no

How Long is It?

Find each object listed on the graph.
Use cubes to measure each object.
Color one square for each cube you use.

Object	Measurement in Cubes									
Crayon										
Pencil										
Glue Stick										
Paint Brush										

1 2 3 4 5 6 7 8 9 10

Use the graph to answer the questions.

1. Which object is the longest? _____

2. Which object is the shortest? _____

3. Which is longer,
   the paint brush or the pencil? _____

4. Which is shorter,
   the crayon or the glue stick? _____

The Shortest Way

Chris and Nikki each go a different way
from the school to the park. Circle your prediction.
Then use a paper clip to measure each way.

Predict: Who goes the shortest way?   Chris   Nikki

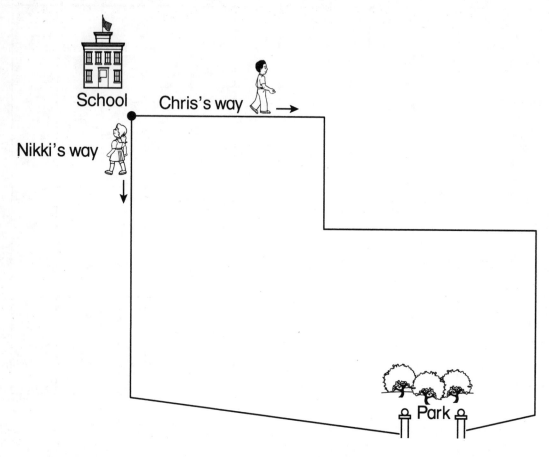

1. Chris's way measured _____ ⬭ .

2. Nikki's way measured _____ ⬭ .

3. Who goes the shortest way? _____

The Inchworm

Each move the inchworm makes is 1 inch long.
The path the inchworm made is shown.
Draw another path the inchworm could have made.
Make it equal in length to the path in the box.

1.

2.

A Foot or More?

Follow each line. Is it longer or shorter than a foot?
Estimate, then measure. Use a ruler.

	Estimate	Measure
1. 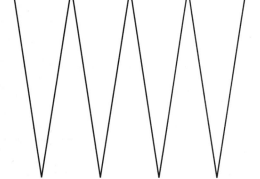	longer shorter	longer shorter
2. 	longer shorter	longer shorter
3.	longer shorter	longer shorter

Measure It!

This is 5 centimeters long.

Estimate if each length is more or less than
5 centimeters. Color a balloon to show your answer.
Then measure.

		More than 5 centimeters	Less than 5 centimeters	Measure
1.				_____ centimeters
2.				_____ centimeters
3.				_____ centimeters
4.				_____ centimeters
5.				_____ centimeters

Around and Around We Go

This map shows two paths.

Path A is the path around the park.

Path B is the path around the garden.

Path A →

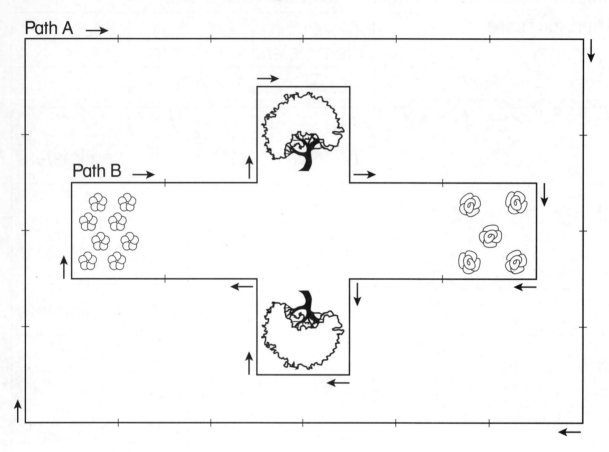

Path B →

1. How long is Path A? _____ inches

2. How long is Path B? _____ inches

3. Which path on this map is longer?

_____

4. How much longer? _____ inches

How Many of Each?

The new floor has 3 different colored tiles.
Choose a color for each of the tiles marked
A, **B**, and **C**. Color the pattern.

☐ ☐ ☐

A   B   C

B	C	C	A	C	C	B
C	C	A	A	A	C	C
C	A	B	B	B	A	C
C	C	A	A	A	C	C
B	C	C	A	C	C	B

1. How many **A** tiles are there? _____

2. How many **B** tiles are there? _____

3. How many **C** tiles are there? _____

4. How many tiles are there in all? _____

Lunchbox Mystery

Use the clues to match each child
with his or her lunchbox.
Then number the boxes from I to 4.
Use I for the box that holds the least.

Marcel   Lee   Sam   Amelia

4 cups

___   ___   ___   ___

Clues:

1. Lee's lunchbox holds fewer cups than Sam's lunchbox.

2. Amelia's lunchbox holds more cups
   than Sam's lunchbox.

3. Amelia's lunchbox holds fewer cups
   than Marcel's lunchbox.

The Lemonade Stand

After the soccer game the children have lemonade. Each person gets 1 cup. Draw a line to match each group to the right amount of lemonade.

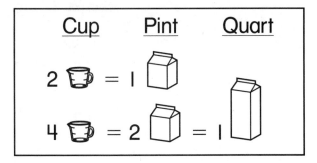

1.

2.

3.

Water Shortage

Think about how you use water.
Circle the best estimate.

1.

    less than 1 liter

    about 1 liter

    more than 1 liter

2.

    less than 1 liter

    about 1 liter

    more than 1 liter

3.

    less than 1 liter

    about 1 liter

    more than 1 liter

4.

    less than 1 liter

    about 1 liter

    more than 1 liter

5. Circle the activity that uses less water.

    or   

  18 liters   30 liters

Balancing Act

Put the number of cubes shown on the scale.

Find an object that will balance.

Draw the object on the right side of the scale.

I.

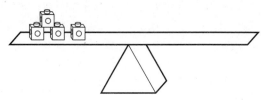

_____

2.

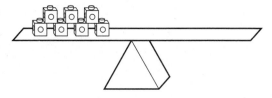

_____

3.

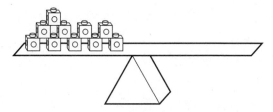

_____

4.

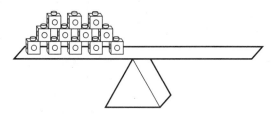

_____

5.

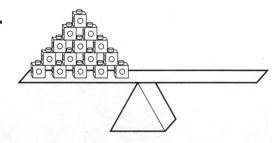

Pack the Backpack

The things in Lisa's backpack weigh about 1 pound each. The things in Rick's backpack weigh less than a pound each. Color Lisa's things red. Color Rick's things blue.

Weighing the Pets

Wendy uses a gram scale for pets that weigh less than a kilogram.

She uses a kilogram scale for pets that weigh more than a kilogram.

Decide which scale Wendy should use for each pet.

Circle your answer.

 = Gram scale

 = Kilogram scale

1.

2.

3.

4.

5.

6.

What Will I Wear?

Look at the thermometer.
Circle what you would wear.

1. 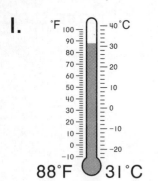 88°F 31°C

2. 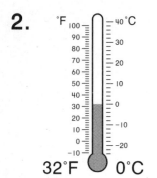 32°F 0°C

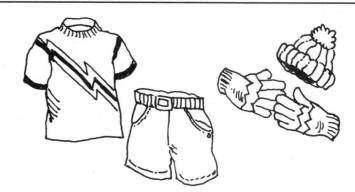

3. 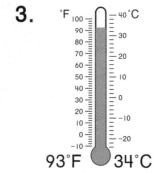 93°F 34°C

4. 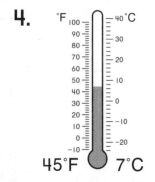 45°F 7°C

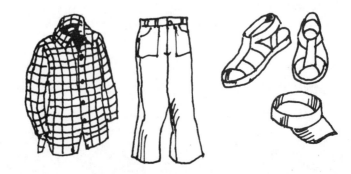

128 Use with Lesson 10-14.

Tool Match

Read each story. Then draw a line to the tool that will help solve the problem.

1. Is the shelf long enough to hold the train set?

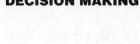

2. Is the water too cold for the fish?

3. Does Julio have 3 pounds of potatoes to make the salad?

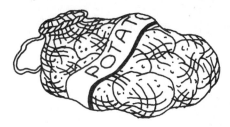

4. How much juice will fill the bottle?

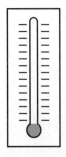

Go Fish

Look at the fish in each tank.
Which fish could you pick?
Circle **certain** or **impossible**.

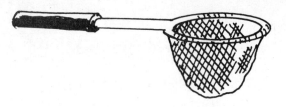

I.

      certain   impossible

   certain   impossible

2.

      certain   impossible

   certain   impossible

3.

   certain   impossible

   certain   impossible

4.

   certain   impossible

   certain   impossible

What are the Chances?

1. Put 9 red cubes and
   3 blue cubes in a large bag.
   Pick a cube 10 times.
   Put the cube back in
   the bag after each pick.
   Mark a tally for each pick.

Color	Tally
Red	
Blue	

Which color are you more likely
to pick out of the bag next? _____

2. Put 8 blue cubes and
   2 yellow cubes in a bag.
   Pick a cube 10 times.
   Put the cube back in
   the bag after each pick.
   Mark a tally for each pick.

Color	Tally
Blue	
Yellow	

Which color are you less likely
to pick out of the bag next? _____

Name _____

Happy Birthday to You!

You are having a party.
6 friends are coming.

1. Circle how much
   juice you should buy.

2. There are 9 banana
   muffins and 3 blueberry
   muffins. Is it more likely
   or less likely that friends
   will get a blueberry muffin?
   Circle your answer.

   more likely

   less likely

3. There are 7 party hats.
   Is it certain or impossible
   that each friend will get
   one? Circle your answer.

   certain

   impossible

4. Each friend brings a gift.
   Tammy's gift is 10 centimeters long.
   Ray's gift is 10 inches long.
   Which gift is longer? _____

5. Your party begins at 1 o'clock.
   It will last 2 hours.
   Your party will end at _____.

Double Up

Read the clues. Cross out numbers
to find the answer to each riddle.

1. I am not the double of 3.
   I am not the double of 6.
   I am not the double of 5.

10	6	16	12

   I am _____ .

   I am the double of _____ .

2. I am not the double of 4.
   I am not the double of 9.
   I am not the double of 7.

14	8	18	4

   I am _____ .

   I am the double of _____ .

3. I am not the double of 8.
   I am not the double of 6.
   I am not the double of 3.

12	8	6	16

   I am _____ .

   I am the double of _____ .

4. I am not the double of 2.
   I am not the double of 9.
   I am not the double of 5.

10	4	14	18

   I am _____ .

   I am the double of _____ .

Double Scoop

Look at the number on the first scoop of frozen yogurt.
Write the doubles fact. Then use the same number to
write a doubles minus 1 and a doubles plus 1 fact.

1.

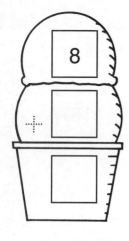
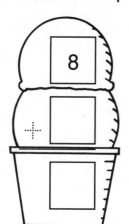
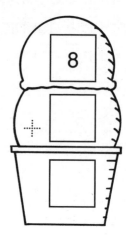

2.

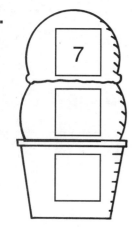
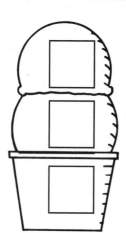
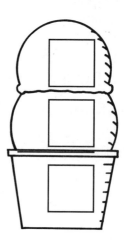

3. Write your own doubles, doubles minus 1, and doubles plus 1 facts.

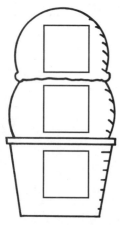
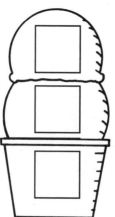
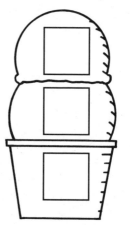

What's Missing?

Draw the missing counters.
Then write the missing addend.

1.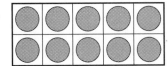

10

+ 5

15

2.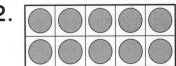

10

+ ☐

14

3.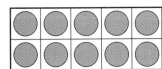

10

+ ☐

17

4.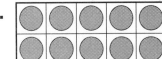

10

+ ☐

13

5.

10

+ ☐

16

6.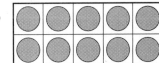

10

+ ☐

18

Funny Money

Write the sums in the first column.

Then match the sums to the coins in the second column.

1. 7¢ + 5¢ = ⎯12⎯ ¢

2. 8¢ + 6¢ = ⎯⎯ ¢   

3. 9¢ + 7¢ = ⎯⎯ ¢   

4. 9¢ + 9¢ = ⎯⎯ ¢   

5. 8¢ + 9¢ = ⎯⎯ ¢   

6. 5¢ + 6¢ = ⎯⎯ ¢   

7. 8¢ + 7¢ = ⎯⎯ ¢   

What's the Point?

Name _____

Name _____

What's the Point?

Each child earns points to use at the second-hand toy sale.

Find 2 toys each child can buy that equals the number of points earned. Use the same color to shade the child and the toys.

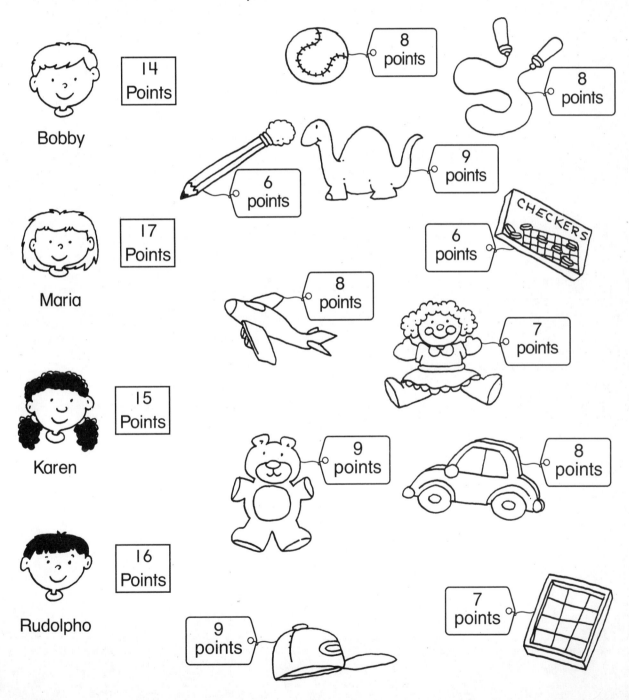

Bobby — 14 Points

Maria — 17 Points

Karen — 15 Points

Rudolpho — 16 Points

How Many is That?

Add the numbers shown.
Circle the two numbers you add first.

1.

$$
\begin{array}{r}
3 \\
0 \\
+ \ 2 \\
\hline
12 \\
\end{array}
$$

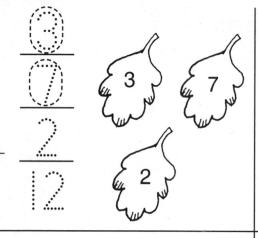

2. _____
_____
+ _____

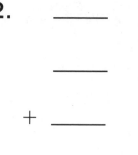 

3. _____
_____
+ _____

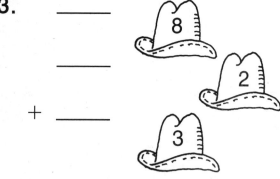

4. _____
_____
+ _____

5. _____
_____
+ _____

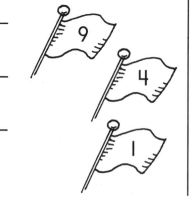

6. _____
_____
+ _____

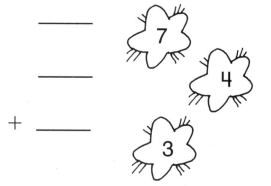

Line up the Animals

You play "Marching Animals" with 3 game pieces.
You have a bird, a cat, and a dog. How many different
ways can you line up these game pieces? Make a list.
Draw a line after each line-up.

First	Second	Third
Dog	Cat	Bird

There are _____ different ways to line up the game pieces.

Are You Related?

Look at the number in the box.

Write an addition fact with that number as its sum.

Then write a related subtraction fact.

1. | 17 |

_____ + _____ = _____

_____ − _____ = _____

2. | 15 |

_____ + _____ = _____

_____ − _____ = _____

3. | 12 |

_____ + _____ = _____

_____ − _____ = _____

4. | 11 |

_____ + _____ = _____

_____ − _____ = _____

5. | 13 |

_____ + _____ = _____

_____ − _____ = _____

6. | 18 |

_____ + _____ = _____

_____ − _____ = _____

Family Ties

Circle the 3 numbers that make up a fact family.
Write the fact family.

I. 4   7   I I   I2   9

___ + ___ = ___   ___ − ___ = ___

___ + ___ = ___   ___ − ___ = ___

2. 7   I3   9   8   I6

___ + ___ = ___   ___ − ___ = ___

___ + ___ = ___   ___ − ___ = ___

3. 6   8   4   I3   I4

___ + ___ = ___   ___ − ___ = ___

___ + ___ = ___   ___ − ___ = ___

4. 8   7   I7   5   9

___ + ___ = ___   ___ − ___ = ___

___ + ___ = ___   ___ − ___ = ___

5. 4   I2   7   3   9

___ + ___ = ___   ___ − ___ = ___

___ + ___ = ___   ___ − ___ = ___

Name _____

Jed's New Pet

What pet does Jed get?

Complete the addition and subtraction sentences.

Draw a line to connect Jed to the related addition

and subtraction facts to find his new pet.

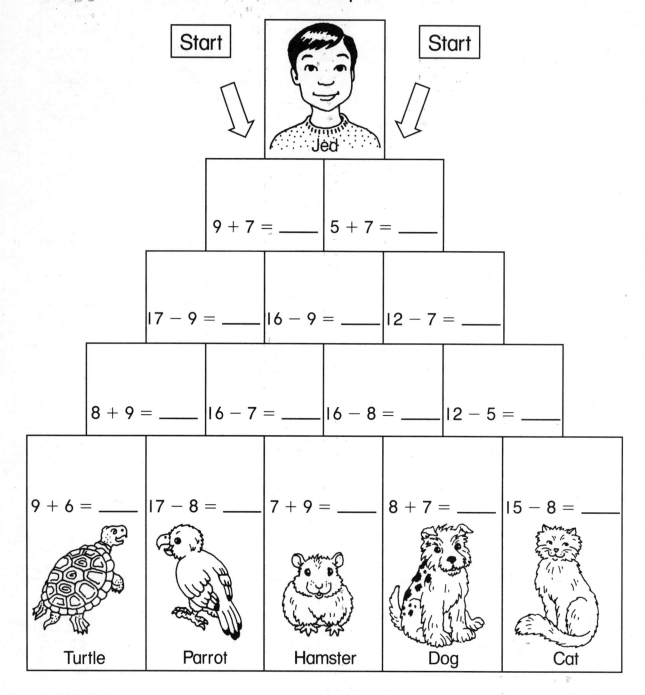

Start

Start

Jed

$9 + 7 =$ _____ $5 + 7 =$ _____

$17 - 9 =$ _____ $16 - 9 =$ _____ $12 - 7 =$ _____

$8 + 9 =$ _____ $16 - 7 =$ _____ $16 - 8 =$ _____ $12 - 5 =$ _____

$9 + 6 =$ _____ $17 - 8 =$ _____ $7 + 9 =$ _____ $8 + 7 =$ _____ $15 - 8 =$ _____

Turtle   Parrot   Hamster   Dog   Cat

Jed got a _____ .

Frame It!

Write the number shown for each ten-frame.

Use that number to write a subtraction fact.

Cross out to complete your fact.

1.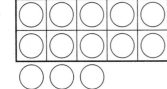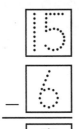

2.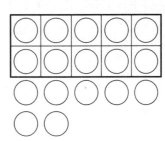

3.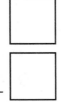

4.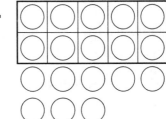

5.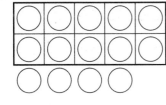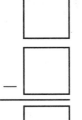

6.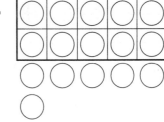

7.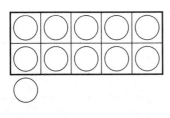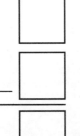

8.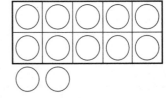

You Name It!

For each addition fact write a related subtraction fact.
Then complete the story problems using the
subtraction facts you wrote.

1. $8 + 4 = 12$

____ – ____ = ____

2. $6 + 7 = 13$

____ – ____ = ____

3. $9 + 6 = 15$

____ – ____ = ____

4. $5 + 6 = 11$

____ – ____ = ____

5. Ann Marie found ____ shells.

She gave ____ shells to Amy.

Ann Marie has ____ shells left.

6. Peter makes ____ muffins.

He eats ____ of them.

There are ____ muffins left.

7. Dan has ____ model cars.

He wants to keep ____ of

them. The rest he gives away.

Dan gives ____ cars away.

8. Rita reads ____ books.

____ of the books are about

dogs. How many books are

not about dogs? ____ books

Pay the Price

Use the price list to answer the questions.

School Store

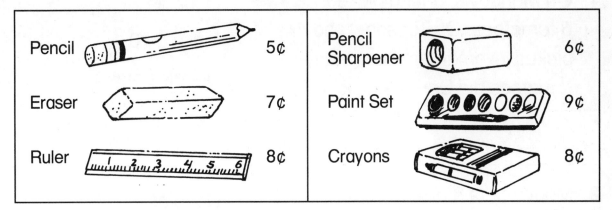

Pencil		5¢
Eraser		7¢
Ruler		8¢
Pencil Sharpener		6¢
Paint Set		9¢
Crayons		8¢

I. Lily wants to buy a pencil and a ruler. How much do they cost?

____¢ ◯ ____¢ = ____¢

Lily pays 15¢.
What is her change?

____¢ ◯ ____¢ = ____¢

2. Morgan wants to buy a paint set and a ruler. How much do they cost?

____¢ ◯ ____¢ = ____¢

Morgan has 9¢. How much more money does Morgan need?

____¢ ◯ ____¢ = ____¢

3. Pam buys crayons and a pencil. How much do they cost?

____¢ ◯ ____¢ = ____¢

If Pam buys the pencil sharpener, how much would her items cost altogether?

____¢ ◯ ____¢ = ____¢

4. Enrique buys crayons and an eraser. How much do they cost?

____¢ ◯ ____¢ = ____¢

He pays with a dime and a nickel. Does he get change back?

____

Use Some Strategy!

Solve. Use the strategies you learned
in this chapter. Circle the strategy.

1. On Monday, Darlene picked
6 tomatoes. On Tuesday, she
picked 7 tomatoes. How many
tomatoes did Darlene pick in all?

   Doubles

   Make a 10

   Doubles plus 1

   _____ $\bigcirc$ _____ = _____ tomatoes

2. Manny puts 8 pigs in a pen.
He puts 4 lambs in a pen.
How many animals did
Manny put in pens?

   Doubles

   Make a 10

   Use addition to subtract

   _____ $\bigcirc$ _____ = _____ animals

3. Carlos collected 14 eggs in
the morning. Some eggs
were used for breakfast.
There are 6 eggs left.
How many were used?

   Use 10 to subtract

   Doubles

   Use addition to subtract

   _____ $\bigcirc$ _____ = _____ eggs

4. Paula picks 6 red peppers,
3 green peppers, and
4 yellow peppers. How many
peppers did Paula pick in all?

   Make a 10

   Doubles

   Doubles plus 1

   _____ $\bigcirc$ _____ $\bigcirc$ _____ = _____ peppers

Dimes and More Dimes

Draw the missing dimes.
Write each number sentence.

1. +  =

$$\underset{¢}{20} + \underset{¢}{30} = \underset{¢}{50}$$

2. + =

_____ ¢ + _____ ¢ = _____ ¢

3. +  =

_____ ¢ + _____ ¢ = _____ ¢

4. + =

_____ ¢ + _____ ¢ = _____ ¢

Circle the two groups that answer the question.

5. Kate has two purses.
She has more than 80¢ in all.
Circle Kate's two purses.

The Missing Tens

The children get points for helping.
Write a number sentence to solve.

1. Eric had 26 points. He walked the dog for Mrs. Jones. Now he has 66 points. How many points did he get?

$26 + \underline{40} = 66$

Eric got $\underline{40}$ points.

2. Marie had 38 points. She fed the baby. Now she has 68 points. How many points did she get?

$38 + \underline{} = 68$

Marie got $\underline{}$ points.

3. Sandy had 42 points. She gave the dog a bath. Now she has 72 points. How many points did she get?

$42 + \underline{} = 72$

Sandy got $\underline{}$ points.

4. Julio had 23 points. He carried food for Mr. Evans. Now he has 63 points. How many points did he get?

$23 + \underline{} = 63$

Julio got $\underline{}$ points.

5. Mike had 17 points. He helped at the library. Now he has 37 points. How many points did he get?

$17 + \underline{} = 37$

Mike got $\underline{}$ points.

6. Tamara had 45 points. She helped weed the garden. Now she has 85 points. How many points did she get?

$45 + \underline{} = 85$

Tamara got $\underline{}$ points.

Add It Up

Color the parts of the rectangle
that equal the sum in the circle.

1. (25)

14	13	11

2. (59)

33	43	16

3. (67)

21	36	31

4. (36)

23	13	26

5. (43)

22	31	12

6. (84)

52	42	32

7. (78)

35	43	25

8. (99)

53	56	46

Name _____

Find the Rule!

Complete the number pattern. Write the rule.

1.

Rule: Add _____		
14	+ _____	22
16	+ _____	24
18	+ _____	26
20	+ _____	_____
22	+ _____	_____
24	+ _____	_____

2.

Rule: Add _____		
25	+ _____	34
28	+ _____	37
31	+ _____	40
34	+ _____	_____
37	+ _____	_____
40	+ _____	_____

3.

Rule: Add _____		
44	+ _____	51
48	+ _____	55
52	+ _____	59
56	+ _____	_____
60	+ _____	_____
64	+ _____	_____

4.

Rule: Add _____		
57	+ _____	63
59	+ _____	65
61	+ _____	67
63	+ _____	_____
65	+ _____	_____
67	+ _____	_____

Make Sense With Your Answer

Read each problem. Circle the best answer.

1. Josh is having a party. He needs to buy
   15 snacks. Each box has 6 snacks.
   How many boxes does Josh need to buy?

          2   3   4

2. Josh needs 3 bags of balloons. Each
   bag costs 22¢. How much money will
   he need to buy the balloons?

         30¢   60¢   70¢

3. Cindy has a photo album.
   She can fit 4 photos on each
   page. How many pages does
   she need for 22 photos?

         5   6   7

4. There are 10 empty pages in the
   photo album. Cindy has 12 more photos.
   How many pages does she need?

         4   3   2

Take Ten

Subtract. Find the missing
tens. Match the missing tens
to the letters in the box.
Write a letter below each
problem. Then solve the riddle.

10	20	30	40	50	60	70
E	T	W	A	O	L	P

1.
$$\begin{array}{r} 50 \\ -\ 10 \\ \hline \square \end{array}$$

_____

2.
$$\begin{array}{r} 60 \\ -\ \square \\ \hline 40 \end{array}$$

_____

3.
$$\begin{array}{r} 80 \\ -\ 30 \\ \hline \square \end{array}$$

_____

4.
$$\begin{array}{r} 40 \\ -\ \square \\ \hline 10 \end{array}$$

_____

5.
$$\begin{array}{r} 70 \\ -\ 60 \\ \hline \square \end{array}$$

_____

6.
$$\begin{array}{r} 90 \\ -\ \square \\ \hline 30 \end{array}$$

_____

Riddle: What gets wetter the more it dries? _____

Problem Solving *Algebra*

7. Write the missing numbers. Then write
the next subtraction sentence in the pattern.

$$\begin{array}{r} 96 \\ -\ 20 \\ \hline \square \end{array} \qquad \begin{array}{r} 76 \\ -\ \square \\ \hline 56 \end{array} \qquad \begin{array}{r} \square \\ -\ 20 \\ \hline 36 \end{array} \qquad \begin{array}{r} \square \\ \square \\ -\ \square \\ \hline \square \end{array}$$

Do The Math!

Write a two-digit number that is greater than the number being subtracted. The digit in the ones place must be greater than zero. Then subtract.

1.

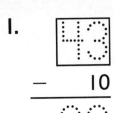

$$\begin{array}{r} 43 \\ -\quad 10 \\ \hline 33 \end{array}$$

$$\begin{array}{r} \square \\ -\quad 30 \\ \hline \end{array}$$

$$\begin{array}{r} \square \\ -\quad 50 \\ \hline \end{array}$$

$$\begin{array}{r} \square \\ -\quad 20 \\ \hline \end{array}$$

2.

$$\begin{array}{r} \square \\ -\quad 40 \\ \hline \end{array}$$

$$\begin{array}{r} \square \\ -\quad 60 \\ \hline \end{array}$$

$$\begin{array}{r} \square \\ -\quad 30 \\ \hline \end{array}$$

$$\begin{array}{r} \square \\ -\quad 20 \\ \hline \end{array}$$

3.

$$\begin{array}{r} \square \\ -\quad 60 \\ \hline \end{array}$$

$$\begin{array}{r} \square \\ -\quad 10 \\ \hline \end{array}$$

$$\begin{array}{r} \square \\ -\quad 40 \\ \hline \end{array}$$

$$\begin{array}{r} \square \\ -\quad 50 \\ \hline \end{array}$$

4.

$$\begin{array}{r} \square \\ -\quad 20 \\ \hline \end{array}$$

$$\begin{array}{r} \square \\ -\quad 30 \\ \hline \end{array}$$

$$\begin{array}{r} \square \\ -\quad 50 \\ \hline \end{array}$$

$$\begin{array}{r} \square \\ -\quad 10 \\ \hline \end{array}$$

Name _____

Make A Difference!

The number in the box is the difference.
Color the circles whose numbers can be
subtracted to get the difference.

I.

12

36   25   13

2.

23

36   59   80

3.

34

65   97   31

4.

13

48   25   35

5.

21

58   37   77

6.

32

85   22   54

7.

14

47   33   45

8.

24

64   88   98

Spending Spree!

Each purse has money in it. Choose one toy
you will buy with the money. Write the name
of the toy. Write a subtraction sentence to
show how much money you will have left.

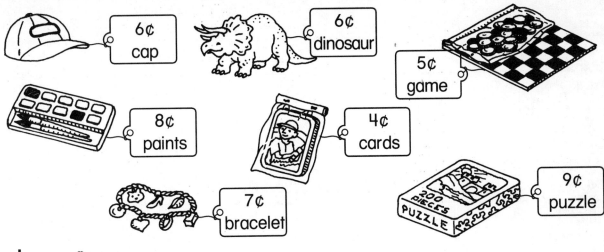

6¢ cap

6¢ dinosaur

5¢ game

8¢ paints

4¢ cards

9¢ puzzle

7¢ bracelet

1. 56¢

_____ ____¢ − ____¢ = ____¢

2. 37¢

_____ ____¢ − ____¢ = ____¢

3. 14¢

_____ ____¢ − ____¢ = ____¢

4. 25¢

_____ ____¢ − ____¢ = ____¢

5. 68¢

_____ ____¢ − ____¢ = ____¢

Graph It!

What color bike do children like the most? Ask
15 children if they like red, blue, or silver bikes the
best. Make a tally. Use the tally chart to make a
graph. Color 1 square for each tally.

		Total
Red		
Blue		
Silver		

Color Bike Liked Best

Red										
Blue										
Silver										

0   1   2   3   4   5   6   7   8   9   10

1. What color did children like the most? _____

2. How many children liked silver bikes? _____

3. Did more children like blue or red bikes? _____

4. What was the least favorite color for a bike? _____

5. Write a question that can be answered using the graph.

_____

_____

Wagons Ho!

Two families are going West. These are the supplies they may take. Each wagon can hold about 100 pounds.

flour
10 pounds

fruit and vegetables
20 pounds

blankets
32 pounds

potatoes
20 pounds

tools
29 pounds

chickens
10 pounds

pots and dishes
29 pounds

clothes
41 pounds

Decide what supplies each wagon will take.
Draw and label them.

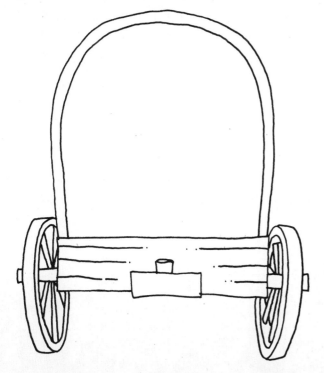

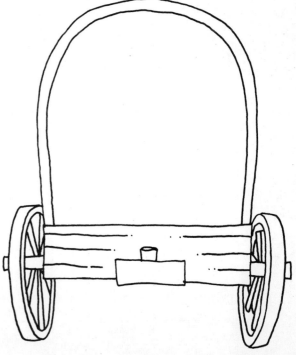